ISBN 0-9707892-0-3

© Copyright 2000

William J. Schauman

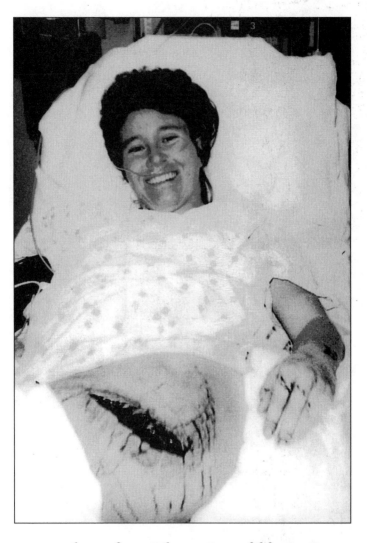

Why is She Smiling?
The true story of a woman and her spirit of survival

Why is She Smiling?

The true story of a woman and her spirit of survival

Edited by Allen Ludlum

Shark Attack Photo on cover
taken by Paramedic Joseph J. Walls
and Paramedic Blake Bartholomew

Cover and Artwork Design by
Dawn Witherington

Dedication

D awn, this is our story. We started our relationship as friends and it developed into
much more. During a very difficult time in my
life, it was your positive attitude and enthusiasm
that helped me discover myself. I am so very
grateful to have met you.

As a testimony of my love, I have decided to
share some of our most intimate experiences
together. Your ability to triumph over personal
tragedy provides an insight into your personality,
and explains why I fell in love.

You and I are the same, and I believe it was
fate that brought us together. You thrive on creating new challenges and enjoy living on the
edge, and to me that makes the future exciting. I
can't wait to see what's next.

Acknowledgment

To my personal friend, Allen Ludlum. I am indebted to you for all your countless hours of proof reading, editing, and assistance with all phases of our project. You were not just a sounding board, you have truly been my mentor.

Robbie, Mort and Sheila thank you for all your help, needed criticism, and encouragement, and to everyone in the Public Safety Department for your patience and understanding during this long endeavor.

Special thanks to my wife, Dawn, Macintyre, Casey, and Keegan for putting up with all the hours spent away from the family.

Why is She Smiling?

Chapter 1

It was September 14th, 1998 and the beginning of a typical evening at the Schauman house. Barbie Dolls, match-box cars, and other assorted toys lay scattered on our juice stained living room carpet. We didn't consider ourselves lazy, but by evening we were both worn out and too tired to clean up. Dawn, my athletic wife of six years, who was thirteen years younger than I, was normally energetic, but now she was nine months pregnant with our third child, and just about ready to deliver. Exhausted from the day's activities, she sat down on our faded worn-out couch to watch television. Macintyre, our active four year old was jumping from one piece of furniture to the next, making it difficult for her to relax, while Casey, our petite two year old, was sitting mesmerized in front of the television with her beloved tattered blanket in hand.

It was 7:30 pm and our plan was to put the kids to bed by 8:00. As I prepared drinks and snacks for the family, Kelli, my twenty-two year old daughter from my first marriage, stepped out of her bedroom to use the phone in the kitchen. She was going out for the evening and looked like a super model with her long blonde hair, hazel eyes and skin tight dress. Kelli moved in with us about a month ago filling our three bedroom home to capacity.

"Where are you going?" I asked Kelli.

As always, she didn't answer me and just rolled her eyes in an unconcerned way.

I had just sat back on our leather recliner, when Dawn got up from the couch and followed Kelli into the kitchen. I watched her as she tip-toed through the toys and clutter, looking uncomfortable and out of proportion with her big belly sticking out from her five-foot-two, muscular frame. Dawn is of Irish descent with long reddish-brown hair, which she normally puts in a French braid, fair skin and blue eyes. She chose to give up a lifeguard career four years ago, when Macintyre was born, to become a stay-at-home mom. She loves it - and shares a very close bond with our children.

As Dawn left the living room, I laid on the floor hoping to keep the kids entertained. Macintyre happily ran towards me with a big grin on his face that resembled his mother's smile. He leaped onto the couch fearlessly and told me to get closer, so he could do a flying knee drop onto my stomach, a game we often played. While this isn't something I'd necessarily recommend for everyone, I manage to keep my six foot frame in good condition, so it's fun for Macintyre and me - especially Macintyre. Casey watched in amusement with her pacifier going a mile a minute. Several riotous minutes passed when suddenly we were interrupted by Kelli.

"Dad, you'd better come! hurry!"

I got up quickly and tripped over a toy, startling the children. Casey started crying. Running into the kitchen, I intercepted Kelli by the phone and knew instantly that something was terribly wrong. I had never seen her look so flustered before.

"I think Dawn's water broke..." she said nervously.

I ran through the master bedroom and into the connecting bathroom anticipating the worst. This feeling of apprehension was a common thing for me living with Dawn. What I saw was worse than I had expected. Dawn was sitting on the toilet holding onto the sides with a pale, weak look on her face, ready to collapse. Blood was everywhere. It's not a good sign when you see blood clots in large quantities. Dawn took one look at me and knew I was worried. She had seen and joked about that concerned look many times before.

Taking a deep breath while trying to compose myself I said, "Dawn, we'd better go - right now!"

"I can't. The bleeding won't stop!" she said. "I need to call the doctor."

I ran to get the portable phone in the bedroom and returned in seconds. I handed her the phone and she started dialing... I started pacing back and forth nervously worrying about her sitting on the toilet so long, fearing that it would make her deliver faster... After several rings, a nurse at the birthing center answered the phone.

"This is Dawn Schauman. I need to talk with the doctor right away. It's an emergency!" Dawn said.

The nurse told her that the doctor would call right back. Almost before she could put the phone down, it rang. Thank God, it was the doctor! I gave a sigh of relief.

"Dawn, what's wrong?" the doctor asked.

"I stood up from the couch and felt something gush out of me. I thought my water broke, but when I reached the bathroom it turned out to be blood. It's pouring out of me and it won't stop! I'm still on the toilet!!"

"How much blood have you lost?"

"I can't tell..."

The doctor asked her to estimate the amount of menstrual pads she would have used to stop the bleeding.

"What do you think, Bill?"she asked me.

"It's a lot... Maybe five pads," I said.

"Probably five pads," she repeated.

"Come to the hospital immediately! I'll be waiting in delivery," the doctor said in an uneasy voice.

Dawn's doctor was normally very self-confident, maybe even to the point of being cocky, but not this time. She had him worried, knowing her history of complications.

I grabbed Dawn by the arm not knowing how stable she was, and tried to hurry her out of the bathroom. She stood up with my help, grabbing a towel off the counter to help control the bleeding. Then she insisted she was Ok. Dawn can down-play any situation.

By the time I hustled her into the foyer by the front door, Macintyre and Casey were both crying hysterically, trying to get to Dawn. They could sense by our anxiety that something was wrong. Kelli was unfamiliar with handling our young children, and although she tried desperately to calm them down, it was obviously difficult for her. I could feel Kelli's stress and see the fear on the children's faces. They were worried, and wanted badly to be comforted by their mommy.

Dawn knew I was beginning to panic, but insisted on bringing the hospital bag she had prepared for delivery. She went back into the bedroom to get her belongings, while I stood impatiently by the front door trying to help Kelli quiet the kids.

Finally, shaking my head in frustration and wondering what was taking her so long, I yelled, "Dawn, what the hell are you doing?"

Shortly after she came out of the bedroom, suitcase in hand.

I've had numerous Dawn experiences before, but this was our third child, the one I thought would be our last. At 45 years of age, those dreams of Dawn and me having a big family of five children got lost in the chaos sometime ago.

Working as a Public Safety officer for years, you'd think that I would have more control, but dealing with family members, and especially Dawn, was different. She's always been a thrill, and definitely knows how to bring the fear out in me. As I rushed Dawn out of the house, her suitcase in one hand and holding her up with the other, I could tell that her condition was worsening. Her skin was turning pasty white and she felt heavier the closer we got to the van. Obviously frightened and concerned for our unborn child, she didn't say a word. When we reached our van parked in the driveway, I pretty much threw her and the suitcase in together. She seemed so little and helpless lying there with her big saucer eyes... I wanted badly to take her place.

"Are you still bleeding?" I asked.

"I think so."

"A lot?"

She hesitated, "I'm not sure."

"It'll be all right, Dawn," I said apprehensively. "Just lie still." I quickly jumped behind the steering wheel. Our house was situated a block from the beach, six miles north of the Sebastian Inlet at the end of the Barrier Island, in a small community called Floridana Beach. We loved the seclusion, but in a medical emergency like this, being thirty-five minutes from the closest hospital was too far. I told Dawn to lie down on the floor of the van with her feet propped up on the seat, hoping it would help.

I backed out of the driveway like a bat out of hell, nearly knocking the mailbox down, and raced down our street at probably three times the 20 mph speed limit. I left Kelli struggling with Macintyre and Casey crying at the dining room window.

I'll never forget that ride as long as I live, and I'm sure Dawn won't either. The van was shaking and rattling. I vaguely remember stopping at the intersection of A1A - at best it was a rolling stop. I hardly looked at the road. Most of my attention was on Dawn lying on the floor of the van.

"Dawn, are you OK?" I repeated over and over.

I felt that as long as she talked to me, she was somewhat stable. We crested the top of the inlet bridge with our wheels barely touching the road, and headed south toward Indian River County Memorial Hospital located in Vero Beach, Florida. At times we were going so fast that it felt like the van was floating. I ran a red light at the intersection of A1A and 510, sped over the Wabasso causeway to the mainland, and rounded the bend on US 1 with the tires of the van screeching and squealing. To me, getting to the hospital as quickly as possible was paramount. Somehow, unbelievably, we reached it without incident. We had made it in twenty-five minutes - record time. I sped up the emergency ramp and stopped in the area reserved for 911 ambulances. After that hell ride, I didn't care what anyone thought.

I jumped out and rushed to the side double doors of the van. When I opened them, Dawn looked up at me with a frightened expression that I'd seen only a few times before. She was going into shock and when I tried to help her out, she collapsed in my arms. By this time, we were beginning to attract a crowd. I stood on the ramp next to the van with Dawn slumped over in my arms, frantically trying to get some medical attention.

"I need help over here!" I yelled.

Several ER nurses rushed to our aid with a wheel chair. I tried to explain in detail what her condition was, but I guess it was pretty obvious. Dawn was certainly pregnant, her color was almost white, and there was blood all over the place.

We rushed Dawn to delivery as quickly as possible, where she was taken to a birthing room for an examination. The room was decorated with oak furniture and fancy curtains, nothing like the delivery room I had expected. A nurse quickly attached a baby monitor to Dawn's stomach, while another checked her vital signs. They didn't say very much, but the puzzled expression on their faces had me concerned. Dawn's obstetrician was on his way, and I was secretly praying that he would commit to a C-section immediately. To this day, I know that Dawn coerced the doctor into believing she was invincible. During her regularly scheduled maternity visits she badgered him about delivering her baby boy naturally. Dawn had a very muscular abdomen from working out and didn't want him to damage it.

For some unknown reason, when Dawn got situated in the birthing room, her bleeding stopped and her skin color returned to normal. She began to take a turn for the better, and all the birthing monitors were indicating that she was having normal contractions. The doctor looked confused as he walked into the room wearing his operating gown. I think he expected Dawn's condition to be much worse from his previous telephone conversation with her. After reading her chart, he decided to give her a very thorough exam, from an internal to an ultrasound. The ultrasound was used to locate the position of the placenta and baby, and any other visible problems. After viewing the ultrasound with the doctor, we both agreed that the placenta looked a little low. The doctor told us that it had dropped since Dawn's last visit, and was now partially blocking her cervix. He explained that this was possibly the reason for some of the severe bleeding. Then, unexpectedly, he gave the thumbs up on a natural delivery. Dawn was elated.

As the doctor was getting ready to leave, he asked her with his heavy New York accent, "Do you want to deliver the baby underwater in a bath tub?"

It's a delivery where a pregnant woman sits in a tub of water, with the doctor close by, as the baby is born. This can be more relaxing for the mother and baby.

"That's totally ridiculous!" I thought.

Fortunately, Dawn said, "No way."

I think we both just wanted to get this whole stressful situation over with.

There we were. I was sitting down wondering what the hell had happened, and Dawn was lying in bed looking pretty calm, as if the evening had been uneventful. She had a happy-go-lucky look on her face that made me wonder if she realized the seriousness of the situation. By the time the doctor left the room, she was actually joking around. Soon, I felt my anxiety begin to leave. Dawn's positive outlook had a way of doing that to me.

We decided to watch television in an attempt to pass the time. For some reason, I can still remember the show that was on, "Mad About You." About forty-five minutes later, we noticed her contractions had begun to subside. Soon after, the doctor reappeared. This time he had an extremely distressed look on his face, and my anxiety returned when he pulled out an eight-inch probe with a hook on the end from one of the wooden drawers.

"What's that for?" I asked.

Concentrating on Dawn's condition he didn't answer me, but I guess the plan was to make sure her water had broken.

I positioned myself behind the doctor so I could see the whole delivery process - good or bad. Dawn was lying down on a bed designed for delivery with her knees slightly bent and her feet flat on the mattress ready for her examination. She looked nervous lying there with nothing on but her hospital gown. The doctor inserted the probe and tugged several times. The room filled with tension... there was an eery silence. Everything seemed to slow down. I watched Dawn's body jerk with the tugs. She grunted as he pulled... making me feel uneasy. Then it happened. The doctor's normally confident face turned white. His expression frightened me. I quickly looked at Dawn - she looked nauseous.

"I feel sick to my stomach. I'm gonna throw up!" she said. She looked like she was in severe pain, and I knew that something was drastically wrong. Then, large blood clots came gushing out.

"Stay with me, Dawn," the doctor said over and over.

Then he shouted, "I need a nurse!"

A nurse came rushing in, looked at Dawn and began to panic. She jumped on top of the bed and tried desperately to stop the bleeding by pressing on Dawn's pelvis.

I turned to the doctor and asked in horror "Is she bleeding out?"

He didn't have to answer.

I asked, "Dawn, are you all right?"

She didn't respond. At that moment, Dawn's and the baby's monitors both went off.

Beep-Beep- Beep!

Beeeeeeeeeep!

Their pulse rate and blood pressure were dropping rapidly, indicating that they were in serious trouble. I felt a hopeless panic run through my entire body.

"Pull the plugs!" the doctor yelled. "We don't have much time."

Before I could pull the plugs, Dawn sat up. She looked at me with an intensity that I had never seen before.

With a piercing stare, she asked, "Is the baby going to...?"

She never finished the sentence. I watched her pass out in front of me. The whole situation didn't seem real. Within a matter of seconds, her skin color changed from a normal, healthy color to an ashen white.

I'll always remember the events of that night like they happened yesterday. We all grabbed a portion of the bed and raced toward the operating room. The doctor was at the head of the bed, while the nurse and I were holding onto the sides. We ran past the maternity floor reception desk, just before we passed through a heavy set of wooden doors that said "No Admittance." The doctor screamed at the nurse behind the desk for additional help and startled her as he slapped the automatic door opener on the wall. She looked stunned. We went through the doors and entered an empty hallway. It was obvious that the hospital staff was caught off guard. To my surprise, when we got to the operating room doors, I was stopped by a large robust nurse dressed in white...

She said in a stern voice, "You can't go in there!"

I wanted to bust into that room along with the doctor... I didn't want to lose Dawn or the baby like this. I needed to be there for them, but something deep inside told me to stop. I truly had faith in the doctor - I trusted him and didn't want to interfere. Dawn explained to me throughout her entire pregnancy about his extensive medical background and how she had confidence in his abilities. Although he only appeared to be in his early thirties, he had initially worked in a busy maternity ward in the Bronx, New York City, where he dealt with every type of OB emergency conceivable. In a situation like this, I felt that he was our only hope.

The nurse that stopped me at the operating room door escorted me back to the birthing room. She didn't say a word as we walked somberly through the empty corridor, but just before I entered the birthing room, she turned to me with a very serious expression on her face, and said, "You need to call Dawn's mom and dad, right now. They should be here."

I knew it was serious, but until that moment, I don't think that I realized the full significance of the situation. It all seemed like a bad dream. I felt like I had been hit by a ton of bricks. Everything happened so fast. The whole hospital scenario to this point was maybe four minutes long, at best.

Chapter 2

I walked into the birthing room in a daze. The door shut automatically behind me. I felt my body trembling as I tried to regain my composure. I needed to call Dawn's mom and dad. It was their daughter and they needed to know about her life threatening condition, but before I could make the call, the heavy wooden door of the birthing room swung open. The nurse from the nurses station was standing in the doorway with a solemn expression. I ran up to her frantically, thinking the worst.

"How's Dawn?"

She didn't answer.

"Are you OK?" she asked.

I sighed, and said, "I'll be all right."

Deep inside, I was hoping the nurse would tell me not to worry about Dawn, that everything would be OK, but she just stared at me, knowing that there was nothing she could do or say to ease my pain.

"If you need anything, just call me at the front desk," she offered.

She had a strained, concerned look on her face, as if she wanted to tell me more, but couldn't.

I asked again, "Have you heard anything at all?"

"No," she said, "but I'll try to find something out."

When the nurse left and the door closed behind her, I broke down and fell to my knees, praying and sobbing. I couldn't stand the thought of losing Dawn or our unborn child.

"Doctor... it's up to you... I have faith in you," I said out loud.

"Why did this happen?" I thought over and over again.

The television was still on, and as I looked up at it, I could visualize the expression on Dawn's face as she lay on the delivery bed, smiling and joking.

"Dawn, you were just here. You were fine."

"I can still hear your laughter."

Again, I tried to compose myself.

I had to call her parents, but knowing her mom was teaching Irish Step Dancing two and a half hours away in Fort Lauderdale, reaching her dad at their home was my only hope. I didn't want to panic him, so I made a conscious effort to stay calm. I took a deep breath and began dialing. The phone rang several times before someone finally answered, but it wasn't her dad, it was her brother Wayne. Dawn came from a family of five, two sisters and two older brothers. Wayne, who was only a year and a half older than Dawn, was living at home with his parents. He and I had become friends over the years, and when he answered the phone, he knew I was upset.

"...I'm at the hospital," I told him anxiously. "Get your dad."

"What's wrong?"

My voice began to quiver with emotion, thinking about Dawn.

"...Dawn's in serious trouble."

Her fifty-three year old, French father picked up the phone. A tool and dye maker by trade, he stood five-feet-six with a stocky muscular frame. An ex-marine and devoted Catholic with very high work ethics and morals, he definitely didn't get rattled very easily. It was about 9:00 pm when I called and he had just gotten home, as he often did after a long day's work.

"What happened?" he asked grimly, knowing that something had gone wrong.

"Dawn's not doing well. She's unconscious, bleeding bad. The nurse said you should be here..."

"I'll be right down," He said in a serious monotone.

I hung up the phone with the thought of him racing to the hospital in the faded green Dodge van that he took such pride in, with over two hundred thousand miles on it.

I stood there by the phone in a trance, thinking about Dawn and all the possible consequences, realizing how quickly life can change. I needed to talk to someone badly, so I called my daughter Kelli. My hands began to shake uncontrollably. Although I tried not to, I cried when I heard her voice.

"I need you... to come down here."

"What's wrong, dad?" Kelli asked in a high-pitched, frightened voice.

"Dawn... might not make it!!!"

There was no response.

"Get the baby sitter," I told Kelli. "She'll watch the kids."

"I'll come right down," she said without hesitation. I love you, dad."

"I love you too, Kelli!"

I hung up the phone, still in disbelief. I desperately needed to hold onto her. I felt alone. Unable to sit still, I began pacing back and forth in the room.

"What am I going to do? I work full time, two young kids... What the hell am I going to do?"

"Maybe Kelli would help."

I knew she would... I caught myself.

"What am I thinking? It's not right!"

"Dawn's the one in trouble and I'm thinking about myself."

"She's going to make it! She has to."

I sat down on the edge of a reclining chair by the window and looked out into the darkness. Working as a Public Safety Officer for fourteen years, and handling all kinds of medical emergencies, I knew the possible dangers to Dawn and the baby... Realizing that they might not live - I felt lost. At any moment, I might have to make a choice. I knew the decision would be Dawn - it had to be. Without her I had nothing. Trying desperately to block out my negative thoughts, I searched for something positive to hold onto.

My thoughts drifted back to when I first met Dawn...

Chapter 3

Iwas driving through the Tracking Station Beach Park in my police car, a silver Ford, Crown Victoria. I had been working for the Town of Indian River Shores as a Public Safety officer for the past six years. Indian River Shores is an affluent, bedroom community located on the Barrier Island in Indian River County, Florida, along the Treasure Coast. It's situated in a pristine area on the beach, where Spanish ships lost their gold and silver treasures in the early seventeenth century, during hurricane season. As a Public Safety officer, I wore three hats; policeman, fireman and emergency medical technician. I worked twenty-four hours on duty and forty-eight hours off. During my shift, I was responsible for patrolling as a policeman for at least eight hours. The rest of the time, I was free to lift weights, run, play basketball, or ride the all-terrain-vehicle on the beach, while waiting to respond to any emergency fire or medical alarm. I really enjoyed my job, especially the life style, having lots of time off to surf and train at the beach.

I parked at the second dune crossover, just beyond the bathrooms. This was my normal spot. The Tracking Station Park is one of my favorite places to patrol in town. It's a quiet, public beach just off State Road A1A, hidden behind a 7-Eleven and Eckerd's drug store at the south end of Indian River Shores. The park butts up against a fenced off annex of the Florida Institute of Technology at the southern end, where biologists study dolphins and other marine creatures, while the northern end borders a vacant five acre wooded lot, making it one of the counties best kept secrets.

I got out of my patrol car and walked toward the second

dune crossover. There are three wooden crossovers in the park that protect the dune from foot traffic, while giving beach goers easy access to the beach. At the end of each walkway is a pavilion, situated high above the beach, allowing spectacular views of the Atlantic Ocean in either direction. As I strolled up the boardwalk, I heard small birds and lizards rustling through the native sub-tropical vegetation, consisting of shrubs, wild flowers, sea oats, and palms. The precious dune that stands twelve feet above sea level, serves as a barrier, protecting the island during storms.

It was fall in Florida. You could tell by the crystal clear, blue sky and low humidity. While standing under the pavilion, I saw that the beach was deserted, except for small groups of sea gulls and pelicans resting on the edge of the surf. As a warm southern breeze from the gulf stream blew across my face, I looked north, staring at the waves and the occasional pods of bait fish passing through. Mullet and sardines followed by sharks, tarpon and other predatory fish were headed south with the warm water, during their yearly migration pattern, signaling that change was in the air - I could feel it and smell it.

The ocean was my life. It was forever moving and changing, and it fascinated me. Sometimes I would just stare at the waves peeling off, trying to visualize how they would end. On my days off, I would sit on my surfboard for hours alone, staring back at the panoramic view of the beach and civilization, wondering about my future. It was like a water meditation. When my surf session was over, I would paddle to shore with a broader perspective of life, feeling a little better about things.

My marriage was over, and intuition told me it was finally time to move on. On this particular day, I needed the ocean bad. It was my refuge. I gazed south toward the lifeguard stand, and noticed a female lifeguard playing near the waters edge. She was wearing a white lifeguard T-shirt and red shorts, covering up what appeared to be a red bathing suit, with a whistle around her neck. It was low tide. She kicked a volleyball in the air,

Dawn at Golden Sands Beach

Dawn at Wabasso Beach

Photographer: John Frazier

bouncing the ball from one knee to the other never letting it hit the wet, hard-packed, sand. She looked like a happy-go-lucky kid. I watched her for a good ten minutes or so, trying not to stare, but I couldn't help myself - she fascinated me. It wasn't just her athletic ability, it was her smile. She seemed so uncomplicated and content just doing her own thing.

I knew the lifeguards were off duty at five in the afternoon, so I rearranged my schedule to meet her. I was back at the Tracking Station at five p.m. sharp. I parked my patrol car next to the only car in the deserted lot, a brown and tan Ford Bronco II with a Florida Manatee tag and a lifeguard sticker on the back - it had to be hers. The sun was hanging low in the sky as I exited my car, giving off an aurora of colors, ranging from red to purple. As I walked toward the southernmost dune crossover, I conveniently ran into her rinsing off at the outside showers. She was wearing a red, french-cut, two piece, lifeguard bathing suit. It was skin tight, and very revealing. As the water splashed against her slightly sunburned body, she appeared much

17

younger and more athletic than I had imagined. She was extremely fit with the strong muscular legs of a dancer and a firm, flat stomach. I leaned against the railing next to the shower dressed like a rugged drill sergeant, with a military style hair cut, gray, short-sleeve shirt, snug dark-blue pants and a gun strapped to my side. She obviously recognized the uniform and very innocently looked up at me and smiled.

"How long have you been working for the county?" I asked.

"About six months," she replied and continued with her shower...

"I've never seen you before," I said.

"I spend most of my time working at the north end of the county, but hopefully I'll get to work here more often."

She noticed me looking at her body and not wanting to embarrass her, I politely looked in the other direction. She finished drying off, as if I weren't there. The temperature was cooling down, so she quickly gathered her belongings, packed them in a duffel bag, and threw on a blue lifeguard sweat shirt, as we both headed for our cars. She opened the rear door of her Ford Bronco and tossed her duffel bag in.

"My name's Dawn," she said. "Where's your station?"

"I'm Bill," I told her. "I work right up the road, two miles north of here."

"Do you come here often?"

"Only when the waves are good," I said. "I like the surf break just north of the park."

"Maybe I'll see you out there sometime," she said.

"Do you surf?" I asked.

"No. I body board."

We said good-bye and both left the park in different directions...

Over the next six months, we slowly got to know each other. I would visit Dawn at her lifeguard tower during work, while checking out the beach, and on my days off, after surfing. At first we'd only talk for a few minutes while she stood on the deck above, never taking her eyes off the bathers.

The Tracking Station Tower stood ten feet above the beach in the middle of the park, just in front of the dune. It had a ladder on the south side that went from the beach up to a small enclosed look-out tower, which was surrounded by a wooden deck with rails. Attached to the tower was a lifeguard safety board, used to alert bathers of current ocean conditions and special hazards, and an eight foot flag pole, jutting out from the rail on the north side of the tower, for warning flags.

During my visits to the tower, I learned very quickly that Dawn was extremely conscientious and loved the physical challenges of life guarding. On her breaks she would train rigorously, swimming, running, and performing various calisthenics. Her routine consisted of sit-ups, push-ups, swimming, and running on the beach in the deep sand. When she got off work, she would eat dinner and go straight to the gym to lift weights.

Eventually, Dawn invited me up into her lifeguard tower. I felt privileged, knowing only certified lifeguard personnel were allowed and, on my days off, I began visiting her more often, staying much longer. We would sit together watching the bathers, talking for hours on end about all sorts of things, but mainly life guarding, the waves, and sports. Dawn was a high school athlete, having received numerous awards and several college scholarships in volleyball, softball and soccer. Throughout our conversations it was obvious that we had a lot in common. She liked working out, scuba diving, riding the waves on her body board - a small, hard-foam board about four feet long by two feet wide - and especially her job. I loved working out and scuba diving, too, but used to kid her about becoming a real surfer, maybe like me. She appeared to have the physical ability, coordination and determination to do any sport well.

Then one day, while visiting Dawn at the tower on the ATV, she asked, "Would you be interested in taking a lifeguard class?"

Her lifeguard instructor certification was ready to expire, and to keep it current, she needed to teach a basic life guarding class. She thought I might be interested, knowing that I spent most of my free time at the beach surfing.

"Yes, I would!" I answered without hesitation.

"The class starts in two weeks... And if you know of anyone else who is interested, let me know as soon as possible."

"I have a couple of friends at work who might want to try it, but I need to get permission from my chief first. I'll get back with you as soon as I get an answer."

Still sitting on the ATV, I revved up the engine, took off throwing sand behind me, and hurried back to the station as quickly as possible, jumping over sand mounds and gullies the entire way. I made it to the concrete bike path, along A1A on the north end of town, in fifteen minutes, sped south as quickly as possible to the station, pulled in the front bay, shut off the engine and went directly into the chief's office. It was a small dingy office with old dark wood paneling and no windows. I barged into the room, and found the chief leaning back in his chair behind an old, eight foot, dark maple desk, rubbing his temples in deep thought. He was a newly appointed chief from Michigan with lots of experience in Public Safety, but unfamiliar with all the issues that could arise working in an oceanfront community. He was a neatly dressed, large, gentle man in his mid-fifties with gray hair, and a very understanding personality - a great listener.

"What's up?" he asked.

"There's a lifeguard certification class coming up in two weeks and I'd like to take it," I said enthusiastically.

"Why would you want to do that?" he asked inquisitively.

"Well, we're surrounded by water with the Indian River on one side and the ocean on the other. We have seven miles of beach and only one guarded access, the Tracking Station..."

He looked at me somewhat befuddled, as if I were from a

different planet.

"We patrol the beach on a regular basis using the All-Terrain-Vehicle... But we have no water rescue capability," I continued.

He sat back in his chair pondering my words, took off his bi-focal glasses, leaned forward, and asked, "Has anyone in the department ever had to perform an ocean rescue?"

"Yes! I have."

Somewhat surprised, he leaned back again with a very curious look on his face.

"Tell me about it."

"One day last year in late August, six months before you arrived, I stopped at the Tracking Station Park while on patrol," I explained. "I was standing under the second pavilion looking at the beach when I heard someone yelling.

'Hey, Bill! Over here!'

I turned quickly and noticed Sammy, a veteran lifeguard of four years, waving his arms frantically, trying to get my attention. I realized something was wrong, so I flew down the stairs barely touching the steps, jumped onto the beach and ran to him as quickly as possible.

'...What's wrong?' I asked.

Red in the face with his voice quivering nervously, Sammy pointed to a swimmer struggling in the surf, and said, 'He's caught in a Rip!'

'...Go get him, Sammy!'

'I can't!'

'What do you mean, you can't?' I asked in frustration.

'I have nine stitches in my arm.'

Confused, but with no time to get an explanation, I shook my head in disgust and took off running toward the struggling swimmer. As I ran for the water with Sammy alongside, I ripped off my gun belt and handed it to him.

'Hold onto my gun and radio, Sammy... and call my station

for help!'

Speechless, he nodded his head. I kicked off my shoes and socks onto the wet sand, but didn't have time to pull off my shirt. I sprinted into the water, high stepping for twenty-five feet by lifting my knees up enough to bring my feet out of the water. When I couldn't run any longer, I dove through the waves. The water was dirty from the heavy wave action which stirred up the bottom, making it difficult to see. I swam using the crawl stroke, with my head partially out of the water, not wanting to lose sight of the victim. He looked weak and was obviously in serious trouble. I swam as quickly as possible toward him, hoping he would stay afloat long enough for me to get to him. I finally reached him at the same time as a concerned surfer, an off duty fireman from the Indian River County Fire Department.

Not knowing exactly what to do, I yelled to the surfer, 'Get him!'

The fireman paddled next to the victim and grabbed one of his arms as I grabbed his other arm. While trying to assess his condition, he went limp in our arms - dead weight.

'Are you OK?' I shouted at the victim.

He didn't respond. His skin was bluish-gray, indicating he was in respiratory distress.

'I don't think he's breathing! We'd better hurry,' I sputtered, treading water and trying to catch my breath.

We both positioned ourselves alongside the victim, then, while using the side stroke with one arm fully extended, and scissor kicking as hard as we could, we awkwardly began towing the victim's heavy, lifeless body to shore. He was an elderly, obese, gray-haired man in his late sixties. At first we tried towing him straight into shore, but didn't make much headway. Realizing we were caught in a rip current, an outward flowing current, we changed directions and began swimming parallel to the beach. It was much more difficult and exhausting than I imagined, but somehow we managed to escape the strong current and made it to shore. It took only a few minutes, but it felt like an hour. By the time we dragged him onto the wet sand, three Public Safety officers from our station were on the beach waiting to take over. Two of our officers quickly took the elderly man from us and laid him flat on his back in the sand. Our lead paramedic kneeled down next to him, put his ear several inches from his mouth and nose, and listened for breath sounds.

'He's barely breathing! Get some oxygen.'

One of the officers quickly put an oxygen mask over the victim's nose and mouth.

'Open the oxygen tank all the way...' the medic shouted while feeling for a pulse. 'His pulse is weak and rapid...We need to get him off the beach... Get the backboard... Let's GO!'

One officer grabbed the wooden backboard that was lying in the sand and quickly positioned it alongside the victim, while another officer and I barrel rolled the man onto his left side. The board was then pushed underneath him, and we rolled him onto it, laying him flat on his back. All four of us strapped him onto the backboard, securing him as tightly as we could so there was no way he would fall off. The paramedic positioned himself by the patient's head, holding onto the front of the backboard, with a second officer and me holding onto opposite sides, and another officer positioned at the foot.

'Ready 1,2,3, lift,' the paramedic ordered.

He was so heavy that we had difficulty lifting him up, as we awkwardly began carrying him toward the parking lot. When we reached the steps, it felt like we were going to drop him, but somehow managed without any problems.

When we reached the parking lot at the end of the dune crossover, the paramedic said, 'Hold on tight. I'll get the stretcher off the ambulance.'

The ambulance was parked close by, with the engine running and the blue and red lights flashing. He opened the rear doors of the ambulance, grabbed the handles of the stretcher and quickly pulled it out, lowering it to a waist high position so the four of us could easily transfer the victim onto it. When the man was secured to the stretcher with another set of straps, he was lifted and placed into the back of the ambulance. I stood at the rear of the ambulance, with my uniform soaking wet, watching the paramedic and two officers as they situated the patient. Our ambulance had the front end of a Ford truck with a large square cab attached to the back, and the same equipment and capabilities as an Emergency Room. The paramedic grabbed the patients left arm and started an intravenous line, while the other officers simultaneously hooked him up to a twelve lead Electro Cardiogram to monitor his heart. Finally, after several minutes of treatment, the patient began to stir and it became evident that his chance of survival had much improved. As the doors shut and the ambulance drove away, I stood there for a few seconds watching and thinking how fortunate the victim had been, knowing that the surfer and I were not trained as life-guards. I returned to the beach to gather my belongings from Sammy. When I saw him standing on the lifeguard tower it made me angry, knowing that he should have attempted the rescue.

'Sammy, give me my gun belt and radio...' I said coldly.

He looked at me with a guilty expression, and handed my gun and radio down to me without saying a word.

'If you can't execute a rescue, you shouldn't be guarding the beach by yourself.'

I left him standing there knowing that I was upset."

I waited for the chief's reaction. After taking it all in, he agreed whole heartedly, and gave me permission to attend the class. He even suggested that other interested officers should attend.

"Thanks, chief. I'll make all the necessary arrangements."

I left his office, jumped into my patrol car, and returned to the Tracking Station. I parked at the first dune crossover and hurried over the wooden planks, under the pavilion, down the stairs, and up to the lifeguard tower... The thought of a new challenge excited me.

"Dawn! Hey, Dawn!"

She noticed me and quickly came out of the tower, but before she could speak, I said, "I've got some great news!"

"What?"

"I got permission to attend your class, along with anyone else who's interested."

"That's great. Do you think anyone else is interested?"

"I know of at least three officers, maybe even four..."

I climbed up the ladder and stood next to Dawn on the deck. We both looked at each other. She could see my excitement.

"What should I do to get ready?" I asked.

She turned to watch several young bathers playing in the surf.

"...It's mostly swimming..." She looked at me again.

"Don't worry, you'll do fine."

Being a surfer and highly competitive, I said, "I can swim, but I don't have any formal training..."

She looked at my body, focusing on my muscular arms and shoulders.

"I've watched you swim in the ocean. You're in great shape."

"Thanks, but I've never trained in a pool," I said apprehensively.

I left the tower knowing that I had something hard to train for.

I tried to patrol, but couldn't concentrate, so I drove back to the station, parked my police car, and went upstairs to the bunk room, the sleeping quarters for officers on duty. Still in deep thought and eager to start training, I changed into my gym clothes, and proceeded to do a two hour, total body workout in the weight room. When I was finished, I showered, dressed, and called several officers who I thought would be interested in the lifeguard class. I managed to round up four, and even arranged for a pool in town where we could train. The residents of Indian River Shores were very supportive of their Public Safety Department and would do anything to help. It was a private pool, hardly ever used, eighteen yards long, and only a quarter mile from our station.

Over the next two weeks, I received instructions from Dawn on different swimming techniques, and trained like a maniac, swimming, running, and lifting weights, in preparation for the class. At six p.m. on the first day of class, we all met at Saint Edwards High School, a private, affluent school on the Barrier Island in Vero Beach that was known for its swimming facilities. It had a twenty-five meter outside pool, large clocks for timing laps, bleachers on two sides for students and spectators, and large locker room facilities for men and women. I went to class casually dressed in a multi-colored, baggy bathing suit and a loose fitting, white t-shirt. We all gathered in a large open hallway just outside the pool. There were sixteen of us, varying in gender, physical condition, and age, from sixteen to forty-seven. We were led into a class room by Dawn and two other instructors. Dawn, our lead instructor, stood in front of the class dressed in her lifeguard attire. She had just gotten off work. Her fair skin looked slightly sun burned, the tips of her weathered reddish-brown hair were bleached blonde from the intense Florida sun, and the scent of sun block permeated the air.

"Everyone take a seat," She said with a big grin.

Dawn had a smile that could light up a room, and when she started speaking, it was obvious she had a passion for her profession.

"Thanks for coming." Dawn said.

The room quieted.

"All classes will be held at this facility. Today we are going to start with an overview of the basic lifeguard class. On your desk you will find a Basic Life Saving textbook and workbook from the Red Cross, and a syllabus outlining the course. We will follow the syllabus as closely as possible. For the first two weeks, we will meet in this classroom for a forty-five minute textbook lecture, followed by practical exercises in the pool."

One of my fellow Public Safety officers cracked a joke and Dawn smiled, but continued on.

"There will be no horseplay around the pool."

The five of us from our department were sitting together in a group, cutting up and making comments under our breath.

"Especially you Shores cops!"

Everyone laughed.

"At the end of the classroom instruction there will be a final test that you must pass in order to complete your certification, along with a practical skills assessment."

Everyone in the classroom was silent.

"I'll run through the list of practical tests that you will be required to execute successfully. First, you must complete a 500 yard swim under ten minutes; second, you must be able to tread water for two minutes, using only your legs, while holding onto a ten pound brick, and ten minutes without a brick; Third, you must be able to submerge to a minimum depth of seven feet, retrieve a ten pound brick, and return to the surface; finally you must be able to perform all the mandatory rescues as required, a cross chest carry, double armpit tow, and single arm tow, while performing Cardiac Pulmonary Resuscitation. There will also be group exercises such as, backboard carries for spinal injuries, and flailing victim maneuvers for those victims who panic and become combative while being rescued, making it dangerous for the rescuer."

The room remained still. It was obvious that some of the students had no idea of the amount of effort and physical training involved.

"Does anyone have any questions?"

Everyone looked around the room apprehensively.

"When do we start swimming?" someone asked.

"Next class, two days from now... We'll start with a class-room lecture, then we'll hit the pool and evaluate everyone's swim stroke... Make sure you wear your bathing suit... Bring a towel, swimming goggles, and don't forget a jacket. It's going to be cool... Any other questions?"

No one responded.

"...Let's take a ten minute break, and when you come back, we'll finish tonight's class by filling out some necessary forms, followed by several mandatory Red Cross videos on water safety and rescues."

We all got up and left the classroom and the silence was broken. Everyone from our department gathered outside in a small group, discussing training strategies and our lack of swimming knowledge. When we returned to the classroom, we filled out all the necessary forms, watched several Red Cross films, and went our separate ways.

The next session came quickly, but having trained hard over the previous several weeks in a pool, I felt somewhat prepared. We all met in the classroom for a forty-five minute lecture, consisting of pool safety, rescue techniques, and a review of the recommended swimming strokes. When it was finished, we were instructed to meet outside by the pool. We all gathered on the bleachers on the west side of the pool. It was an open area with no protection from the wind, over-looking a field that led to the Indian River. The sun was beginning to set and there was a chill in the air, so we all huddled close together on the metal benches trying to keep warm, waiting for our instructions. Dawn came out of the class-room several minutes later and quickly began organizing the class.

"We'll start by picking partners. There will be two of you assigned to one lane. The lanes can be set up for twenty-five yards or twenty-five meters. To make it easy for counting laps, we've set up the lanes for twenty-five yards. You will swim 500 yards using whatever stroke or strokes you feel comfortable with... That's ten fifty yard laps. For those of you who can't add, that means you must swim twenty-five yards to the far end of the pool, then twenty-five yards back, for one lap. It will be timed, but before we start, we'll demonstrate all the strokes; crawl, breast, back and butterfly. Any questions?" Dawn asked.

One young student nervously asked, "What if we can't make it under the ten minute time requirement?"

"Try your best, this exercise is for practice only, and it will give us a chance to evaluate your level of conditioning and stroke."

I chose Nat as my partner, a friend and fellow officer from the Public Safety Department. His job was to count my laps, then vice-versa.

"Everyone who's elected to go first, line up on the edge of the pool," Dawn instructed.

I was going first from our team.

"There will be no diving into the pool tonight, so please step in and get ready."

I jumped down into the water and adjusted my goggles... Everyone looked tense. The whistle blew. I felt my adrenaline pump as I quickly kneeled down underwater, and sprung off the side of the pool as hard as I could. With my arms fully extended, I glided through the water holding my breath for several seconds, then popped to the surface and started swimming, using the crawl stroke. My strategy was to swim at a steady pace, using good form the entire way. It was difficult for me though, being so competitive and knowing I was being timed. Five laps passed and I felt pretty good, then eight.

"Seven minutes!" Nat shouted. "You can do it!"

Knowing that I only had two laps left, I tried to push myself. I stroked harder and harder until, finally, I touched the wall for the last time. I popped up out of the water and ripped my goggles off.

"What's my time?"

Dawn looked at her stop watch, "Nine minutes..."

"Alright!" I responded.

With my muscles pumped and still tight from the swim, I placed my hands on the concrete deck and lifted myself out of the pool in one motion. What a rush, I thought to myself.

Next it was Nat's turn. He had a large muscular frame with the arms and legs of a weight lifter. Determined, he jumped into the pool and got ready. The whistle blew and he took off at a very quick pace. For the first two laps he looked great, then he began to tire. On his fourth lap, he had to stop by the edge of the pool to rest.

"Don't quit, Nat!" Push yourself!" I shouted.

He took off again, but this time, with a new understanding of his physical limitations, he swam at a much slower pace. On the sixth and eighth laps, he had to stop again. Then with sheer determination, he muscled his way through the ninth and tenth laps. When he touched the side of the pool for the last time, he looked completely worn-out and was obviously relieved. Swimming was definitely a lot harder than either one of us had anticipated.

The class ended shortly after our 500 yard swim, so I gathered my belongings from the bleachers, threw on my sweat shirt and headed to my car. I timed my walk so I would meet Dawn halfway out to her car.

"Hey, Dawn. Fun class tonight."

"What was your time?" she asked inquisitively.

"You told me nine minutes."

"Good time."

"Thanks!" I said. "But I still have a lot to learn."

Dawn recognized my competitive spirit, so she stopped and gave me some pointers.

She turned toward me and said "To improve your time, your

arms need to extend out from your shoulders as far as you can reach."

"I don't understand."

"You're not extending them all the way. You're bending your elbows and not following through. At the end of each stroke, your hand should be fully extended by your thigh."

"What about my kick?"

"You have what I call a surfers kick. Your legs are too far apart, your knees are slightly bent, and your right leg kicks awkwardly out to the side."

"How should my legs be positioned?"

"Keep them close together, with your knees locked and your feet fully extended. When you kick, your energy should come from your thighs, kicking straight up and then down. It's called a flutter kick."

I nodded my head.

"Your body needs to glide through the water effortlessly."

She started walking toward her car again.

"Thanks, Dawn. Maybe I'll see you at the beach tomorrow... I'm on duty."

"That's great," she said, and waved good-bye.

Over the next several weeks, I worked diligently on improving my swim style, and would visit Dawn on my days off for personalized instructions. She was extremely helpful, and on her breaks, we would spend time together swimming in the ocean, critiquing each others strokes. We would swim seventy-five to one hundred yards out, just beyond the breakers, in about eight feet of water. On clear days, when the visibility underwater was ten feet or more, I would position myself beneath the surface as she swam by, evaluating her every move. She looked so smooth and graceful as her young, muscular body glided by me with perfection. As she reached forward during each stroke with her hand cupped, her body would rotate as she pulled her arms through the water, propelling herself forward. The entire time her legs flutter kicked like a machine, leaving very little splash. Watching her swim was definitely the highlight of our training and a great learning experience.

During the fourth week of class, we started reviewing different rescue techniques. I vividly remember the first night of practice. It was a perfect night to be outdoors with temperatures in the low seventies and not a cloud in the sky. We all gathered on the bleachers anxiously waiting to start. Listening to the conversations, it was obvious that over the past three and a half weeks, there was a lot of mutual respect and camaraderie built up amongst us.

Dawn stepped out onto the pool deck wearing her red, two-piece lifeguard bathing suit, carrying her goggles in her left hand.

"Everyone find your partner and gather around me by the pool," Dawn said.

We quickly formed a semi-circle around her.

"Tonight's training, and all other single-person rescues will take place in the deep end of the pool. During this particular training exercise one student will pretend to be a swimmer in distress, while the other will perform a cross chest carry. This is probably the most common rescue performed without a rescue buoy" (a flexible foam floatation device, used to keep a victim afloat). "The rescuer will jump into the pool, swim within six feet of the victim, make verbal contact in an attempt to calm the distressed swimmer, and then tow the victim to safety towards the shallow end."

Dawn put on her goggles and jumped into the deep end of the pool... We all gathered closer to the edge.

"I need a volunteer..." she said, while treading water...

"Someone who knows how to perform the rescue... I want to go through the rescue procedure slowly, so everyone can see the maneuver."

"I'll do it!" I said.

"Remember, take your time. This is not a contest."

I jumped into the pool and started swimming toward her with my head out of the water, trying to maintain eye contact the entire time. When I got within several feet of her, I stopped. Then, using the rotary kick, a swimming technique used to stay stationary with your legs twirling in opposite directions like an egg beater, I tried to get her attention.

"Calm down! It'll be Ok," I said to Dawn with a smile.

She was frantically splashing at the water with her arms, pretending not to listen.

"Calm down!" I said again, rolling my eyes sarcastically.

Everyone in the class laughed at our role playing, but she still pretended not to listen.

"She's not going to make this easy," I thought to myself.

I dove underwater and came up two feet behind her. Quickly getting my bearings, I went underwater again, but this time when I came up, I grabbed her under her armpits with both hands. Then with my thumbs pressed against her back and my four fingers under her arms, I kicked as hard as I could, lifting her torso slightly out of the water and quickly throwing my left arm across her chest, clutching onto her opposite side with my hand. Once Dawn was situated lying on her back with her head out of the water, I began towing her to the shallow end of the pool, using the side stroke and modified scissor kick. This was the first time since meeting Dawn that we made physical contact with each other.

When I finished with the rescue and let go of her, she turned to me, smiled in a flirtatious manner, and said, "Not bad for a beginner."

"Yeah, right!" I responded.

When the class ended that night, I left thinking about Dawn... Was there something possibly developing between us? I wasn't sure, but for the first time I could feel something.

At the beginning of the next-to-last class of the session, we all gathered in a group by the bleachers, discussing the possibilities of a celebration. Someone suggested that we meet at a restaurant for pizza and beer after the last class, and we all agreed.

The last class came quickly, and I was anxiously waiting to swim the 500 yard, timed event. I wanted badly to improve my nine minute time to eight. Thanks to Dawn's confidence in me and a lot of training, I thought it was possible. Finally it was my turn. I lined up on the edge of the pool on the outside lane. The lanes were marked with rope and small white buoy's every ten feet.

"Everyone get ready," Dawn said.

I adjusted my bathing suit and goggles and got into a squat position. In anticipation of the whistle, I began swaying my arms back and forth - I was ready.

Beep, beep!

Dawn blew the whistle. A surge of energy rushed through my body as I plunged into the pool, hitting the water with my arms fully extended. I felt the water flow by me as I flutter kicked for ten feet underwater. When I surfaced, I instantly began swimming, extending my arms in front of me with every stroke, pulling with everything I had. I followed the black lane marker beneath, as my body moved through the water with ease. Everything felt right, and before I knew it, the lane marker ended and it was time to flip turn and head in the opposite direction. Holding my breath, my right arm extended in front of me, I pulled down hard, throwing my legs over my head, doing a front somersault. My feet flipped over my head hitting the side of the pool with perfect timing. Then, pushing off the wall and twisting at the same time, I headed effortlessly in the opposite direction.

The first five laps went by like a flash, and when I pushed off the wall on my sixth lap, I heard someone yell, "Five minutes left!"

I swam even harder, believing I had a good chance of making it in under nine minutes.

"One lap to go!" someone yelled.

I sprung off the wall for the final time with only twenty-five yards left, came up, took a deep breath, and stroked as hard as I could, holding my breath the entire time. When I touched the wall for the last time, I popped to the surface gasping for air and completely spent.

"Seven-forty-five!" Dawn yelled.

Elated, I vaulted out of the pool, and began rejoicing with several of my fellow students. It was finally over and it felt great, knowing that I was able to meet the physical challenges of the class.

When the session ended, Dawn called us to the bleachers and began handing out our lifeguard certificates individually.

"...Mike!" she said, shaking his hand. "Good job."

"Mark, I don't know how you made it, but good effort."

Everyone laughed, knowing how difficult it was for him on the 500 yard swim.

"Bill, all right!" she said, slapping my hand in a high five fashion.

After she handed out the last certificate, she said, "I want to congratulate everyone for a job well done."

We all applauded.

"Who's going out tonight?" Dawn asked.

Ten of us responded cheerfully.

"I'll meet you in the parking lot by my car when you're done getting ready," Dawn said.

We all left for our respective locker rooms, showered, dressed, and regrouped in the parking lot.

"Why don't we go to Crusty's," Dawn suggested. "It's close by, and has great pizza and draft beer."

Everyone agreed. Crusty's was a small restaurant with an ocean view just a few miles north of Saint Edwards High School, at Humiston Park, Vero Beach.

We met in the parking lot of the restaurant and walked inside together as one big group.

"How many in your party?" a waitress asked.

"There's ten of us, and if it's possible, we'd like to sit together," I said to the waitress.

"Sure, that won't be a problem," she responded, and began pushing several tables together.

"Can I get you any drinks before you order?" the waitress asked.

"Let's get some beer!" someone shouted.

Everyone of drinking age threw a couple of dollars on the table.

"We have draft beer," the waitress said.

"We'll take two pitchers," Dawn said.

When the beer arrived, we began celebrating our accomplishments, reminiscing about all the events that had taken place in the class. Several toasts were made by students thanking the instructors, and especially Dawn, for their hard work and dedication. Then we all pledged our friendship and success for our future as lifeguards.

After finishing our pizza and beer, I said, "Let's continue our celebration at the beach."

"Good idea!" someone answered.

"Why don't we go to the Tracking Station Beach. It's only a couple of miles away and it's very secluded." Dawn suggested.

We all agreed.

"I'll pick up some beer and snacks at the 7-Eleven and meet you inside the park," I said.

We said good-bye to the underage students, then got in our cars and left.

It was about 9 o'clock when we finally made it to the beach. The park was already closed, but we went in anyway. It was a perfect night for a lifeguard celebration with the temperature in the lower seventies and no bugs. We parked our vehicles at the second dune crossover. It was pitch black, except for the stars flickering in a cloudless sky.

"Does anyone have a flashlight?" someone asked.

"Shhh! Be quiet," Dawn said. "Someone might hear us."

No one had a flashlight, so we crept slowly, feeling our way toward the pavilion, trying to keep quiet. As we crossed over the dune I could see a sliver of the moon beginning to appear on the horizon. We climbed gingerly down the stairs to the beach without making a sound. The night was unusually still, and the ocean was extremely calm. We headed north, a hundred yards past the last pavilion, and picked a cozy spot in front of a vacant five-acre lot. We sat down in the darkness halfway between the ocean and the dune. The only sound that could be heard was the ocean lapping peacefully against the beach. When we felt that it was safe to talk, our silence was broken with the sound of a beer bottle being opened. Everyone laughed and the celebration began.

Several hours passed quickly. I remember sitting in the sand in a trance, staring at the ocean, thinking about diving in.

"Let's go swimming!" I suggested.

"We can't," Someone said. "We don't have our bathing suits."

It was obvious no one felt like going back to their vehicles to get their swim suits, so I stood up and started walking toward the water.

When I got about fifty yards away, I yelled, "I'm going in!"

Everyone was silent until I began taking off my clothes.

"Wahoo!" someone yelled.

Naked, I took off running toward the ocean and dove into the water. When I surfaced, I turned toward the beach. To my surprise, everybody, except Mike, a fellow Public Safety officer and friend, had stripped off their clothes and were running toward me. They hit the water hooting and hollering. It was great.

Not wanting to be the only Public Safety officer in the water, I yelled to Mike, "You better get in the water, now! You're making me look bad."

It didn't take much to coerce Mike into the water. He quickly took off his clothes and dove in.

We swam out into the warm ocean without a care in the world - what a thrill! Eight months ago I felt content just existing.

"Not now," I thought.

It reminded me of my high school days, and I felt alive again, wanting more out of life... Then without warning, Dawn jumped on my back. I'll never forget that moment as long as I live. My heart was pounding with excitement as her young body pressed against mine. It was an incredible feeling being 100 yards out in the ocean treading water with her wrapped around me.

"Am I dreaming?" I thought.

The only light was from the moon and stars reflecting on the water.

"Can this actually be happening?"

...I felt guilty with her being so young.

"What could she possibly see in me?" I thought. "Dawn and me together... Is it possible?"

Dawn held on to me tightly. The intensity was overwhelming! Suddenly, a light appeared on the beach and Dawn quickly let go. It was Joe, a sergeant from my department.

Not wanting to explain myself I said, "swim out."

Without hesitation, we swam out as quickly and quietly as possible, just out of range of his flashlight. We waited silently with our bodies suspended in the water, until finally, he was gone.

"Let's get out of here," I said.

We all swam to shore as quickly as possible, and when we

reached the beach we scattered in different directions scurrying to get our clothes on. When we were all dressed, we headed back to our vehicles. Then Joe and another officer intercepted us halfway to the stairs.

"What were you doing? he asked me in a sarcastic tone.

"Oh, nothing," I answered. "We just graduated from life-guard class and wanted to have some fun."

We kept walking as if nothing unusual had happened. He didn't ask any more questions, but the smile on his face said it all.

Dawn and I left that night in different directions. By the time I got home, my head was spinning. I couldn't get her off my mind, and I fell asleep realizing she had everything I secretly desired. The next day I rushed to the beach, climbed up into the lifeguard tower to see Dawn and looked deep into her eyes. She was difficult to figure out, but there was something there - we both could feel it... Standing on the deck we embraced, then kissed. Fortunately, no one was on the beach so it went un-noticed. Flustered, Dawn and I quickly went into the tower and sat down staring at the ocean, holding hands.

"I'm totally attracted to you," I told Dawn.

She held onto my hand tighter, but didn't say anything.

"I can't get you off my mind."

She turned and looked at me, and I melted into her arms again.

When we let go this time, I said, "I want to know everything about you."

"Ask me anything," she said softly.

"Why did you jump on my back last night?"

"It was an accident," she said with a smile.

"Then why didn't you let go?"

She didn't answer, so I changed the subject and asked about her family.

"Where do your parents live?"

"Fort Pierce, near Indian River Community College."

"Do you have any brothers and sisters?"

"I have two brothers and two sisters. Someday, I would like you to meet my family, especially my parents," she said. "I know they'd like you."

"Why do you say that?" I asked.

"They're full of energy and very outgoing - just like you."

We spent the rest of the day learning everything we could about each other.

My next day off, I met her at the lifeguard tower on her lunch break. She was so excited to see me that she jumped down from the tower and gave me a big hug. We walked holding hands toward the edge of the ocean. Dawn looked very attractive in her lifeguard bathing suit. It had to be the same one she wore the first day I met her.

It was a beautiful day, and the aqua colored water was so clear that we could see the outline of the reefs in the distance. The Tracking Station has three sets of reefs that run parallel with the beach. The first one starts a hundred yards out, in about ten feet of water, and the last one ends a quarter mile out, in twenty-two feet of water. The ocean was flat, perfect for swimming. We walked into the water slowly, just staring out over the ocean. Suddenly, trying to get a head start, Dawn dove in, swimming as fast as she could away from me. I jumped in after her, trying to catch up, but she was an extremely fast swimmer. Dawn loved to be chased. Finally, after we were two hundred yards out, she let me catch her. I grabbed onto her tightly, tickling and squeezing her, trying to make her laugh.

"Stop it! Stop it!" she said out of breath.

I let go.

"Let's swim to the pier and back," she said.

The pier was old and abandoned, and at least eight-hundred yards south of the lifeguard tower.

"Are you kidding?" I said. "I'll never be able to keep up."

"Yes you..."

Before Dawn could finish her sentence, I took off swimming. We raced for a hundred yards, then stopped to rest. After a few minutes of treading water, we took off again. We swam non-stop for seven hundred yards until we were ten feet from the pier. The pier stood thirty feet above us, extending out a hundred yards from the beach, with pilings the size of telephone poles.

"Let's swim under it," Dawn suggested.

I agreed and followed her as she maneuvered through the oyster riddled pilings to the other side. When we made it through, we decided to sit on the beach and talk for a few minutes before heading back. We swam to shore and walked under the pier to a secluded spot on the beach. We collapsed next to each other, lying flat on our backs in the sand, staring at the sky.

After lying there for a few minutes, Dawn said, "I want to try surfing."

She was a lot like me and willing to try anything.

"I would love to teach you, but we'll have to wait until the waves pick up."

Just the thought of Dawn surfing excited me. We both stood up, brushed off the sand, then ran to the water, dove in and swam non-stop back to the tower.

It was summer in Florida and the only chance we had for a swell to develop was from a tropical depression or hurricane passing by. After several weeks the waves started to pick up. They were created from a small tropical storm developing in the Caribbean. The next morning at nine o'clock sharp, I was at the beach with my surfboard in hand. I surfed in front of the tower until Dawn's break. Finally she waved me in. I could see the enthusiasm on her face as she ran down the beach to greet me - she was so excited. I laid my board down in the hard packed sand.

"Let's go!" Dawn shouted.

"First, I need to wax my board," I told her.

It was similar to candle wax, applied to the surface of the board so your feet wouldn't slip.

Dawn kneeled down next to me as I began rubbing the wax on.

"The first thing you have to learn is how to balance yourself on the board while you paddle. It's a lot harder than it looks. The key is not to get too far back on the board."

Dawn had been watching surfers since she started guarding, and had a general idea what to expect.

"I can only give you pointers. The rest is up to you."

Dawn picked up the leash that was lying in the sand and put the velcro strap around her right ankle. The leash was attached to the surfboard so you wouldn't have to swim after it once the wave ended. It was also a safety feature, so unsuspecting bathers wouldn't get hit by a loose board. She picked up my six foot, eleven inch surfboard. It was a foam board with a wooden stringer in the center, covered with several layers of fiberglass, with a fin attached to the bottom for turning. We entered the water with the sun shining and a slight breeze coming out of the southeast. The waves were about two feet high, measuring from the back, perfect for her first day. She walked into the warm water until she was waist deep, then placed the board down and laid on top of it.

I swam along side as Dawn paddled on my surfboard - she was a natural and had no problem balancing herself.

"When you see a wave coming, try to paddle as fast as you can. When you feel the wave begin to push you forward, try to stand up in one motion. Your feet should be about shoulder width apart, with one foot in front of the other."

Her experience body boarding was a great help. She lined herself up in perfect position with a wave behind her, and paddled as fast as she could. The wave picked her up and pushed her forward as she glided down the face of it. Then in one motion, she jumped up onto the board with her left foot forward. She stood up so fast that she got tossed head over heels into the water, nearly getting hit by the board. Dawn was actually too aggressive.

"Take your time!" I yelled."Don't stand up until you're stable!"

The next wave came and she got thrown off her board again. I laughed, and she gave me a nasty look. Dawn was very determined and would slap and punch at the water at her own inabilities, and I learned quickly to look in the other direction. Finally, after a couple more wipe-outs, she was able to ride a wave the entire way to shore.

"Hoo Hoooo!" she yelled excitedly as she finished her ride. She was ecstatic, grinning from ear to ear, and waving at me.

"I did it! I did it!"

Acknowledging her ride, I shouted, "All right!"

Being able to surf together was definitely a turning point in our relationship and made our bond stronger.

Chapter 4

A week after Dawn learned to surf, a friend of mine from the Eastern Surfing Association, a small organization that sponsors surf contests for young people all over the country, asked me to chaperone a surf trip. He wanted me to help him with a small group of surfers from the east coast on a trip to Costa Rica. I didn't agree right away, but after sleeping on it, I decided to go. Dawn and I seemed perfect for each other, but I felt it would be a good opportunity for me to get away and think. I was married to my first wife for a long time and was apprehensive about another long term commitment.

Was it finally time to move on? I felt like I was ready, but I wanted to be sure.

In the past, surfing big waves seemed to clear my head, and the trip to Costa Rica sounded perfect.

The day before I was supposed to leave, I rode the Public Safety ATV up to the Tracking Station lifeguard tower to visit Dawn. She had no idea I was leaving, and I had to say good-bye. As I drove up, Dawn was surrounded by a large group of seagulls flying around. Suddenly, she caught one, and showed it to me with a big beautiful smile on her face. She was so irresistible that I felt weak inside. I invited her for a ride on the ATV.

Photographer: John Frazier

Dawn after catching a seagull

Dawn feeding the seagulls

"Dawn, we need to talk."

"What's wrong?"

"Nothing. Just get on."

She jumped on the back of the ATV and held onto me tightly. As we rode south toward the pier, I wondered what she was thinking. She sensed something was bothering me and I didn't want to upset her. Finally, I stopped the ATV in an isolated area just before the pier and we both got off. I looked into her young beautiful eyes.

"What is it?" she asked.

"You know how I feel about you."

She looked at me with a worried expression on her face, and nodded her head.

"I've decided to take a surf trip to Costa Rica."

She looked surprised.

Bill and Dawn at Tracking Station Beach

"When?"

"Tomorrow."

She turned away from me, obviously disappointed.

"I'm going for ten days with my son, Billy, and a group of surfing champions from the Eastern Surfing Association. They've asked me to chaperone, and I thought it would be a good opportunity to get away and think."

"...I guess I understand," she said.

We both got on the ATV and headed back toward the lifeguard tower.

When she dismounted, it just came out of my mouth,

"Would you like to go with me?"

"I can't... Besides, you need to be alone,"

I felt guilty, knowing it was all so sudden. We hugged for a few seconds, then she turned and ran to the tower.

I left the next day for Costa Rica with my heart aching. From the moment that we landed in San Jose, Costa Rica, I couldn't get Dawn off my mind. The following morning, I was sitting on my surfboard a half-mile out, in Boca Barranca, a small town on the west coast of Costa Rica famous for it's long left point break.

It was a perfect day for surfing with huge glassy waves rolling in from the Pacific. The waves would begin breaking at the river mouth, then peel to the left for at least a quarter of a mile, with perfect form. I sat in the water staring at the mountains off in the distance, wondering about our relationship, trying to put things in perspective.

We started as friends and it had developed into much more. It was like a light that came on in my head, and I realized that I had to take a chance, we were so right for each other. Suddenly my concentration was broken. I looked toward a cliff that jutted five hundred feet straight up out of the water on the south side of the river mouth, and noticed a giant wave coming. I began paddling farther out, trying to get in the best position possible to catch it. I didn't want to get caught in too close on a wave that big - it could be dangerous. The wave got closer. It was enormous, and I badly wanted to ride it. I lined myself up with it directly behind me, and started paddling with everything I had. I felt the wave pick me up... then looking straight down at an eighteen foot wall of water, I jumped to my feet and took off. I rode the wave for three hundred yards maneuvering and pumping my legs the entire way until my thighs were burning. When the wave ended I paddled to shore, knowing that my decision would be to take a chance. Without Dawn, my life would not be complete.

The rest of the trip went by quickly, and when we returned, I couldn't wait to see her. I dropped Billy off at his mother's house, and rushed to the Tracking Station in my red, Ford Ranger, pickup truck. I felt like a young man again. I parked, jumped out, slammed the door, and ran as quickly as I could to the lifeguard tower. When I crossed over the dune, Dawn was standing on the deck watching several bathers. She had no idea that I was coming.

"Hi, Dawn!" I yelled as I jumped off the steps onto the sand. Dawn turned toward me and her whole face lit up. She jumped down from the tower, and ran to me with arms wide open. As we embraced, I picked her up and spun in a circle.

Still in my arms, she asked, "How was your trip?"

"It was fun, but I missed you badly... I love you, Dawn, and want to be with you forever!"

She looked stunned for a moment, then said, "I love you, too!" and buried her head in my chest.

Over the next couple of months both of us felt like we were on an emotional seesaw. When I was with her, I felt a passion and intensity that was beyond my wildest dreams, and when we were apart, I was devastated. Finally, after several months, we decided to live together.

She was renting a small one bedroom apartment on Azalea Lane in Vero Beach, two miles south of the Tracking Station, and I was living with my sister Sandee, in Floridana Beach, fifteen miles from town. It was an easy choice. I packed my bags and moved in with Dawn the next day. It was great. We were finally together and it felt right. We worked out, surfed, ate... and talked for hours on end.

Chapter 5

I t was three days before Thanksgiving, and Dawn and I wanted to do something special on our first holiday together.
"Let's take a trip to the mountains," I suggested. "Have you
ever been to Gatlinburg, Tennessee?"

"I went there once with a church group in the summer,
when I was younger," Dawn said. "But it's been so long I can't
remember too much about it."

"I've never been there," I responded. "But a friend at work
told me it's a great place for a romantic get-a-way."

Gatlinburg is located in the heart of the Smokey National
Forest, surrounded by large mountains with quaint wedding
chapels, and picturesque chalets scattered over the mountain side.

"Let's go!" Dawn said enthusiastically.

We decided to make it a long weekend, hoping to find a
chalet hidden in the mountains. Dawn and I put in our vacation
requests at work, and luckily got permission to leave the next
day. That night, we went to bed at nine, wanting to get an early
start in the morning. We woke up at five, threw on our clothes
and began packing our bags.

"Bill, do you think I'll need a winter coat?" Dawn asked.

"I'm taking mine. It'll be cold at night."

It was still dark when we stepped outside, and the night sky
was filled with stars flickering in the distance, with the temperature in the upper sixties. We quietly walked out to the parking
lot, threw our bags in my pickup, and took off. The thought of
being alone for four days in the mountains excited us. We drove
northbound on I-95 with no itinerary, no reservations, and no
special plans. It was invigorating knowing I was with someone

so spontaneous. We sped through Florida, talking about all sorts of things, and before we knew it, we were in Georgia stopping for gas.

"I think we need a map," Dawn suggested.

"What for? We'll find it. Besides, does it really matter where we end up?"

The weather was already changing, with the temperature dropping as Dawn ran into the store for drinks and snacks.

On her way out, she found her sweatshirt in the pickup, and asked, "Are you cold?"

I was standing outside in my t-shirt, pumping gas and said, "I'm freezing. Could you get my jacket and baseball hat?"

We took off again heading north, turned west onto I-26 in South Carolina, and drove straight through to the mountains. When we reached Asheville, North Carolina we turned onto I-40, a winding, four-lane truckers route that passed by the Great Smokey Mountains.

We saw signs for Gatlinburg, so we stopped at a welcoming center near Newport, Tennessee.

I walked up to the information counter and asked the lady attendant for directions.

She handed me a map, and asked, "Do you need anything else?"

"Yes, do you know if there are any chalets available in Gatlinburg?"

She laughed.

"This is one of the busiest holidays of the year. The rentals have been booked solid for months."

Realizing how disappointed we were, she said, "I can check to see if there are any cancellations. That's your only hope."

"Thank you," I responded.

She got on the phone and made some calls.

Then with a surprised expression on her face, she held her hand over the receiver, and said, "There might be one available.

A couple has backed out of their reservation because they felt the road to their chalet was too steep."

She got back on the phone again, said thank you, and hung up.

"I can't reserve it for you, but if you hurry, it should be available."

"All right!" I responded. "Thanks for all your help."

She gave us directions to the rental office and we took off.

We made it to Gatlinburg in just over an hour. The street lights were decorated with Christmas ornaments, and the road was lined with small shops, restaurants, and all sorts of interesting attractions, including wedding chapels. As we drove toward the rental office, we noticed the town was situated at the bottom of a large mountain. We saw a large gondola packed with tourists headed to the top of Ober Gatlinburg, a ski resort located on the top of the mountain with an indoor skating rink, restaurants and amusement rides.

We drove through town, made a right hand turn at the last numbered light, and headed up the mountain. It was five in the evening when we finally pulled into the rental office, a small A-framed chalet, located right next to the road, that had been converted into an office, We parked our truck, crossed our fingers for good luck, and went inside.

The front door opened into a small, ten by ten, knotty-pine, office. The room was empty when we went inside. I rang the bell on the counter, hoping we weren't too late... No one responded. I rang it again, and a well dressed woman in her mid-forties appeared.

"Can I help you?" she asked.

"Yes. A lady from the welcoming center said that you might have a chalet available," I said hopefully.

She slowly flipped through her registration book.

"You're in luck. We had a couple cancel several hours ago."

"We heard the road was very steep."

She drew open a shade covering a window to the parking lot.

"Is that your pickup?"

"Yes it is."

"You shouldn't have a problem. There's only one bad spot on the road. As you get near the top, there's a hairpin turn that is very steep. Just take your time."

Overjoyed, we agreed to take it, and because it was so late in the day, we were even given a discount.

She handed us two keys, and said, "There's wood on the porch. Make sure you open the flu before you start a fire."

"Is there a grocery store on the way?" I asked.

"No, you'll have to go back down into town."

We went back down, got some groceries, then anxiously headed for our chalet. We made it with no problem, although our wheels did squeal on several of the sharp turns. When we saw the chalet, we were elated. It was an older, three-story, wood-framed house, nestled between large hickory, maple and oak trees. It had a balcony, large stone fireplace, four bedrooms, and a terrific view of the town below.

It was getting dark and cold by the time we finished unpacking.

"I'll get the firewood and kindling, if you get the matches," I told Dawn.

I went out to the woodpile on the deck that surrounded the house, and gathered some wood, while she found some matches in one of the kitchen drawers.

"I saw some charcoal and lighter fluid in one of the cabinets so there must be a grill outside," she said.

"Great!" I responded, stoking the fire, while Dawn turned on the heater and opened the curtains to the giant windows in the living room. The view was breathtaking. We went outside onto the deck and stood next to each other, staring at the twinkling lights below. I could see Dawn's breath as the smell of oak burning permeated the cool mountain air. Starting to get chilled, we went back inside to warm up.

"I'm going upstairs to take a hot shower," Dawn said.

"That sounds like a good idea. Let's grill some steaks when we're finished."

It felt great as I stood there soaking in the hot water. When I stepped out of the shower, I heard a loud crackling sound coming from the fireplace, so I wrapped a towel around my waist and went to investigate. Dawn had already finished and was lying next to the fireplace on a large fluffy, love seat. Her naked body fascinated me and I was taken by her natural beauty.

"How can I be so lucky?" I thought.

It reminded me of the first time I had seen her on the beach, kicking that volleyball in the air. We spent the rest of the night enjoying just being together, lying in each others arms, planning our future.

Dawn and Bill in Gatlinburg, Tennessee

Over the next several days, we hiked in search of waterfalls and played in the Great Smokey Mountains. At night, we would head home, start a fire and collapse in each others arms again.

On the last day of our vacation, we decided to visit Sliding Rock Falls, a waterfall that flowed over smooth rock, cascading several hundred feet down, emptying into a crystal clear pool of water. It was a cold, blustery, overcast day when we arrived, with the temperatures in the upper forties - definitely not a day for swimming. As we pulled into the parking lot, we could hear the river roaring. It was about fifty feet across, partially hidden under the limbs of large oak trees with magnificent white pines, maples, and a variety of other hardwoods. Rocks and boulders of all different shapes and sizes lined the riverbank leading to the main rapid near the center. Dawn kneeled down and touched the water.

"It's ice cold... I wish it was summer."

She wanted badly to slide down the falls.

"Our wetsuits should be behind the seat," I said.

We kept them in the truck during the winter, for cold surfing conditions.

"I'll go check and see if they're still there."

I ran back to the truck and found them tucked behind the seat.

"Hey, Dawn." I yelled, holding the wetsuits in the air. "Let's go!"

Her whole face lit up. We quickly went to the restrooms and changed.

Dawn stepped into the freezing, cold water as I followed close behind. We jumped from one slippery rock to the next, balancing ourselves, trying to work our way out to the rapids.

"Whoa!" I shouted, with my arms fully extended, almost falling off a rock. "Dawn, do you think it's safe?"

Before she could answer, I watched her fall into the river on her butt. She tried to get back up, but the current was so swift that she was swept down the falls.

"Dawn!" I shouted helplessly.

"Whoa! Whoa!" she yelled, as she bounced down the rapids,

hitting one rock after another.

There was nothing I could do to help, so I quickly worked my way out to the main rapid, jumped in, got myself into a sitting position with my feet in front of me, and slid down the falls behind her. When I splashed into the ice cold pool at the bottom, it took my breath away. I popped to the surface, and found Dawn playing and splashing in the water as a group of tourists looked on in disbelief... If you could have seen the look on their faces. They must have known we were in love.

We got out after a few minutes, quickly toweled off, put on our warm clothes, and ran to the truck. We jumped in and turned the heater on full blast. We sat huddled next to each other, shivering and laughing the whole time. On our way home, we passed several wedding chapels.

"Dawn, let's get married."

Totally surprised, she asked,"Are you kidding?"

"No, I'm not. You know I love you."

"I love you too, but I want my parents at the wedding."

"But it's so beautiful up here," I said."We can break the news when we get home... Then we could have a big reception with our family and friends."

Dawn looked tempted...

Flustered, she said, "You're crazy."

"Ok, maybe I am, but when we get back, I want to get engaged."

"Is this a proposal?" she asked.

"I guess it is."

Dawn accepted.

The next morning we woke up with the peaceful sound of a cool, steady rain falling on the roof. It was so cozy lying there with her in my arms snuggled underneath the blankets, that it was difficult for us to leave, but we had to. Reluctantly, we packed our bags, ate breakfast and left for Vero Beach. The winding roads were slick as we slowly made our way down the steep mountain. As we pulled away from Gatlinburg, we made a promise to each other to come back in the future.

I turned east onto I-40 with Dawn's head lying against my shoulder as she snuggled next to me.

Just before she fell asleep, I suggested, "Let's get married on the beach. I know a great spot with a pavilion."

Dawn looked up at me with her sleepy eyes and said, "I love the springtime. Let's get married sometime in April."

Spring was a beautiful time of year in Florida with cool evenings and warm, sunny days. We envisioned a beach setting with family and friends and the sound of the waves lapping in the background. As we continued to plan for our future, the eleven hour trip to Vero Beach flew by, and before we knew it, we were home.

It was still light when we pulled into the apartment complex parking lot. As we got out of our pickup the muggy conditions felt stifling. Dawn and I quickly unpacked our bags and changed into something light.

"I need to exercise after that trip," Dawn said. "Let's go for a run."

Stretching my stiff legs, I said, "I can't wait to see the ocean."

We put on our running shoes and jogged north on the bike path along A1A, turned right at Jaycee Park and headed south onto the boardwalk. The beach was vacant and the ocean was extremely calm. We continued our run down Ocean Avenue, then turned west toward home and ended our forty-five minute run at Riverside Park.

As we cooled off walking down Azalea Lane, I said, "I'm glad to be home."

Dawn agreed.

"I'll make dinner so you can relax," she said. "After all, you did all the driving."

Shortly after dinner I fell asleep next to Dawn, watching television. I felt totally content, thinking about our trip to the mountains, and our future together.

On my next day off, I picked Dawn up after work. She had just finished rinsing off when I pulled up, and expected to go straight home.

"Dawn, let's pick out your engagement ring."

She was completely surprised.

"Are you sure?"

"Did you think I was kidding? Let's go."

She threw her duffel bag in the back and we headed to the Melbourne Mall.

We spent several hours looking at all sorts of rings, until finally, we both agreed on one. It had a small, round, diamond setting with a gold and black antique band, and came with a matching set of wedding bands. I wanted our engagement day to be a surprise, so I didn't buy it right away and somehow managed to put it on lay-away without her knowing.

One week before Christmas, I went back to the mall while she was working, and picked up her ring. My plan was to formally propose to her on Christmas Eve. She knew that we were getting engaged, but wasn't sure of the date.

Christmas Eve came quickly and, after dinner, we both sat down on our living room couch listening to Christmas carols on the radio. Our living room was small with the dining room attached to it. The Christmas tree stood in front of a sliding glass window that opened onto a second-story, outside walkway. It was a freshly cut Douglas Fir, decorated with lights, tinsel, and a star on top. The smell of the tree permeated the room.

"Let's exchange gifts tonight," I suggested.

We took turns getting our presents out of their respective hiding spots. I went into the bedroom and brought out two large clothing boxes wrapped with red and green Christmas paper, ribbons and bows, and placed them on the coffee table. All the lights were turned off except for the Christmas tree. Unbeknownst to Dawn, I had her special gift in my pocket.

"You go first," I said.

She unwrapped her presents rather quickly and smiled graciously, but I could see she was secretly disappointed.

"Now it's your turn," she said.

I opened my presents and thanked her. We both hugged and kissed for several moments.

"Oh, I forgot to give you something, Dawn."

"What?"

"I have one more present for you."

I reached into my pocket and pulled out a small gift box. Dawn's face lit up with joy. She sat back, opened her present and held her engagement ring in her hand with tears in her eyes.

"Before you put it on, let me have it," I said.

I dropped down on one knee, held the ring in my hand and said, "Dawn, will you marry me?"

"Yes," she said softly.

Chapter 6

My thoughts returned to Dawn lying in the operating room unconscious. I could feel her helplessness. I wondered why I hadn't heard anything about Dawn's or our baby's condition.

"What's taking so long? I can't wait much longer," I said in frustration.

Distraught, I walked over to the television set, turned it off, and sat back down.

"What's happening, Dawn? ...I need you."

"Don't leave me now... Don't give up!!!"

I looked toward the ceiling, closed my eyes, and again, began to reflect on our relationship.

Chapter 7

It was April fourth and a beautiful spring day in Florida. The sun was shining brightly, with a crystal-clear, blue sky and temperatures in the upper seventies. The top was down on my old, white, convertible MG as I sped north on A1A. I was dressed in a black tuxedo, my hair was cut short, and I had on my favorite black sunglasses. The warm spring air felt great as it whipped by my face and through my hair. Today I was marrying Dawn.

I was thinking how fast my life had changed - well, maybe it wasn't that fast. I went through years of loneliness. I believe it was Dawn that finally gave me the inner strength to move on.

The closer I got to Floridana Beach, the more I thought about her. It was her whole demeanor. She always had a positive attitude, never complained, and, most of all, never held a grudge. When she got angry, she would tell you what was on her mind, and that was the end of it. Soon after she was back to normal, smiling and enjoying life.

As I crossed over the Sebastian Inlet Bridge, a structure built years ago that traverses a man-made inlet dividing Indian River County from Brevard County, I saw seagulls, pelicans and osprey flying overhead. They looked so graceful and free with their wings spread open, gliding through the air.

"Dawn has changed my life," I thought to myself. "When I'm around her, I feel free to express myself without worrying about any repercussions."

I arrived at the Floridana Beach pavilion at twelve-forty-five, fifteen minutes before our wedding. A crowd of friends and family had already begun to gather. Floridana is a small community six miles north of the Sebastian Inlet in Brevard County, located on the barrier island with the Atlantic Ocean on the east side and the Indian River on the west. The weather was perfect, with a slight breeze coming off the ocean. I stood near the pavilion, an open wooden structure situated on the dune amongst wild vegetation. It was fourteen feet long, overlooking the ocean. The waves were less than two feet high and were breaking close to the beach. Several families were hidden under umbrellas as fishermen stood casting their lines into the surf, and young bathers swam and played in waist high water.

I looked toward the small cinder block club house, and saw my son, Billy, and my daughter, Kelli. Billy was eighteen years old, six-feet-two, very muscular, had hazel eyes, and bleached, blonde hair from the sun. He and I were very close and would surf together several days a week. Kelli was sixteen years old, five-feet-eight, and very shapely. She and I loved each other very much and shared similar personalities.

It was very important to me to have their blessing, and to keep them involved in my new life. The three of us had gone through a lot of family trauma during my divorce, and I was extremely concerned about maintaining a positive relationship with them. While Billy and Kelli were supportive of Dawn and me, I don't think they truly understood why we were together; and probably wouldn't until they had experienced some serious relationships themselves.

Standing near the folding chairs that were set up behind the pavilion in the grass, I began to socialize with family and friends. It was interesting. Members of our families looked apprehensive, but our friends knew that Dawn and I were right for each other. She was my true friend, and, because we were so much alike, I think she understood me better than anyone else in the world.

Dawn arrived and the crowd became silent - she looked perfect. She was wearing a beautiful white dress with a matching

WARNING
Sea Turtles Are
Protected By Law
Report Distracted
Hatchlings Or
Anyone Molesting
Eggs Or Hatchlings
Sea Turtle

Billy and Kelli at Floridana Beach on our wedding day

white hat. She had a giant smile on her face, and walked toward the pavilion like a woman who was sure of herself. She was absolutely stunning! It was her strength and conviction throughout our intense relationship that confirmed my decision to be with her.

I met Dawn halfway down the path and held her hand. We looked at each other and smiled. This was our day. We walked past our friends, now seated, went under the pavilion and stood in front of the minister, looking toward the east - the ocean was our life. My brother, Nick, my best-man, was standing next to me, along with my dad, mom, Billy and Kelli. Next to Dawn was her sister, Chanda, the maid-of-honor, her dad, mom, brothers Wayne and Dale, and her sister Colleen. Dawn and I looked at each other. There was complete silence except for the sound of the waves lapping on the beach. I concentrated on Dawn and looked deep into her soul - she was so happy.

"Marrying Dawn... It just doesn't seem real," I thought.

Our wedding day

Photographer: Laurie Burdette

Time seemed to slow down. I can't remember hearing all the ministers words. Staring into Dawn's beautiful eyes put me in a trance.

"Dawn, I will take care of you forever..." I said to myself.

Our wedding day

Photographer: Laurie Burdette

The ministers words broke my concentration.

"...Until death do you part!"

"I will," I said.

The minister turned to Dawn.

"....Will you, Dawn, take Bill to be your lawful wedded husband... In sickness and in health... until death do you part?"

"I will!" she said.

We were finally together... forever!

After the ceremony, we took photographs under the pavilion, then stood on the walkway shaking hands and hugging everyone who stopped by to congratulate us. We talked to family and friends for over half an hour before we decided to leave. When the last car pulled out of the parking lot, we jumped into our convertible MG and headed south on A1A toward our reception. Several months earlier, I had reserved the Indian River Shores Community Center for the celebration. It was located next to the Public Safety Department, where I was stationed. It seated up to seventy-five people, and was situated in a cosy hammock of large oak trees surrounded by plush green grass. We crossed the Inlet bridge oblivious of our surroundings, totally concentrating on each other.

When we arrived at the community center and walked through the double doors, everyone stood up and clapped. The room was decorated with white streamers hanging from the ceiling fans, and the head table was set up across the far end of the room, facing everyone. We were escorted by my brother to our table as everyone continued to applaud. The tables were arranged in rows, leaving a center area open for a small dance floor. Each table had a center piece decorated with white and blue balloons, and champagne glasses for everyone.

We sat down at the head table with the sound of champagne bottles popping. My brother stood up and silenced the crowd.

"I'd like to make a toast..."

He turned and looked at me.

"At your first wedding I was the ring bearer, and now I'm the best man."

Everyone laughed... He held up his glass.

"Working at the Public Safety Department, I watched Dawn and Bill get teased unmercifully. If they can handle that kind of abuse, they must be meant for each other... To the best matched couple that I know, I wish you both a long and healthy life together."

Everyone cheered and drank their champagne, then started tapping their glasses with their spoons, demanding that we kiss. I gave Dawn a passionate kiss that lasted for at least twenty seconds. Everyone started clapping and whistling, and the celebration began.

Dawn and I ate, danced, and socialized with our family and friends until dark. It was like we were entertaining our friends at home. We actually were the last to leave, and after saying good-bye, we jumped into our MG and drove straight to our apartment. Our plan was to leave on our honeymoon early in the morning, so we quickly undressed and began packing our bags. My dream had come true! Finally, I would get to take Dawn to Costa Rica. It wasn't the typical honeymoon, but neither was anything else that we did. Our itinerary was to surf, eat, ... sleep, and do it all over again for ten days straight.

At five the next morning, we loaded our pickup with two suitcases full of bathing suits, T-shirts and shorts, then went back and got our surfboards. To prevent any damage that might occur on the trip, we packed them in specially made surfboard carriers that had a pliable, hard-plastic coating on the outside and a soft, fabric lining on the inside. For extra protection, we also stuffed clothing around our boards and Styrofoam over the fins. There was no way we were going to Costa Rica with damaged boards; besides, in a third world country, it would be difficult to get them repaired.

We made it to the Miami airport in two and a half hours and

pulled up to the Lasca Airlines departure gate. We got out of the pickup, unloaded our surfboards and bags, and I drove to the long term parking garage while Dawn stayed with our luggage. I returned as quickly as possible, and we both carried our surfboards and bags to the check-in counter. When the automatic sliding glass doors opened to the airport lobby, it was like we had arrived in Costa Rica - everyone was speaking Spanish. At the counter, a crowd of people were staring at us inquisitively. I don't think they were used to seeing a woman carrying a surfboard. We checked our bags in without any difficulties or delays, and departed right on schedule.

It was a two and a half hour flight to Costa Rica, a small third world country located in Central America, with Nicaragua to the north and Panama to the south. It's known for it's friendly people and magnificent landscape, from active volcanos to tropical rain forests. I personally loved its secluded, pristine beaches and great waves. To me, it was like having the best of both worlds, with warm tropical conditions, big waves and a view of the majestic mountains in the background.

From the time we landed in San Jose, the capital of Costa Rica, it was an adventure. San Jose is the largest city in Costa Rica situated on top of a volcanic mountain range. We got off the plane and were shuttled through a busy corridor, then down a flight of stairs where people were lined up slowly being checked in through customs. The building didn't have air conditioning, and we were both sweating from the humidity. After presenting our proper identification and filling out the necessary paperwork, we were escorted through another hallway, then into a large stuffy lobby with no windows. People were everywhere, yelling and scurrying in all different directions - it was definitely a mob scene. We squeezed our way to an antiquated conveyor belt and found our luggage, then began searching for our surfboards. After several minutes, an attendant wheeled an old dolly into the lobby with several large packages on it and our boards tucked underneath. We grabbed our boards, got in line, then passed through yet another check point. We made our way up a flight of stairs to another crowded lobby, and waited for a few confusing moments before I noticed a man neatly dressed in a flowered print, short-sleeve shirt and long pants, holding up a sign that said, "The Schaumans."

"Over here," I yelled through the crowd.

We made eye contact and he quickly made his way to us.

He grabbed our suitcases, and said, "Follow me."

He pushed his way through the crowd and took us outside to a parking lot filled with rental cars. The sun was shining brightly with the temperature in the mid-eighties.

"What type of vehicle do you want?" the attendant asked.

"A four-wheel-drive pickup, with an extended cab," I said.

The roads in Costa Rica were very rough and mostly dirt, and in some of the more remote areas, the only way you could get around was with four-wheel drive. He walked us to a red Toyota pickup.

"Will this do?" he asked.

"That's perfect," I responded.

He wrote down our credit card number and scrutinized the vehicle, noting any existing damage.

"It's yours," he said, handing me the keys and a carbon copy of the paperwork. "Where are you going?" he asked.

"Jaco Beach," I replied.

"Do you need directions?"

"No, I've been there many times before."

We threw our bags in the back seat and placed our surfboards into the bed of the pickup. It was four feet long so our boards stuck out over the tailgate. When the attendant walked away, two young teenagers approached us and asked if we were interested in exchanging money. One American dollar was worth somewhere between one hundred and forty to one hundred and fifty colones, depending on who you exchanged your money with.

"I'll give you one hundred thirty-eight colonies for one dollar," one of the boys said.

I shook my head as if we were not interested and said, "Not enough."

He pulled out his calculator and the two boys spoke to each other in private.

He turned to me and said, "One hundred and forty."

I looked at Dawn as if I knew what I was doing, and pulled out forty dollars from my pocket.

"One hundred forty-five," I said.

The two boys looked at each other again, smiled, then nodded their heads in agreement. Forty dollars was a lot of money in Costa Rica and when the market conditions were right, they could make a nice profit on the exchange. The teenager with the calculator quickly punched in the figures and showed me what the exchange rate was worth in colonies.

We made the exchange, and when we were finished, he asked, "Do you have any surf stickers?"

Surf stickers and t-shirts were very popular with the locals.

We handed them several stickers, jumped into our pickup and took off toward Jaco Beach, a small exotic village centrally located on the Pacific west coast, surrounded by large mountains and known for its fun waves. Leaving San Jose, we drove for about ten minutes on a paved, two-lane highway through a rural area, before it turned into a narrow, winding, dirt road. As we maneuvered our way through the mountains, we passed by one small village after another. Children would rush to their picket fences as we drove by, waving to us as their parents apprehensively looked on. It was obvious that they lived a very simple life and were not used to seeing strangers. Their housing was modest at best, and they wore very plain clothing that appeared to be home sewn. Every yard was packed with chickens, pigs, and goats, and had a well attended vegetable garden and plush beds of flowers. I blew the horn as we were being chased by small children waving and dogs barking. Sitting there next to Dawn, I felt like Harrison Ford in "Raiders of The Lost Ark." I was the richest man in the world.

Halfway to Jaco, we stopped at a small general store with an old fashioned Coke-bottle thermometer hanging alongside the door. As we pulled off the roadway into a small dirt parking lot, a mother hen with her tiny chicks scurried to safety, squawking the entire way. We walked into the old wooden building not knowing what to expect. When we opened the door a middle-aged woman, with her two small children stuck to her side, stood behind the counter while a skinny black and brown dog milled nervously around.

"Hello," I said with a smile. "Do you have any cold drinks?"

She looked at me with a blank stare, not understanding a word I said. I pointed to an advertisement for Coke on the wall. She nodded her head while pointing to a small refrigerator standing against the wall, and said, "Si."

Remembering some of her Spanish from grammar school, Dawn said, "Gracias."

I took two bottles of Coke out of the refrigerator. They were the old style coke bottles with long glass necks and bottle caps that had to be opened with a bottle opener.

When I placed them on the counter with some other snacks, the woman pulled out a small calculator from a shoe box filled with money, and said, "Three hundred and fifty colonies."

After paying and saying good bye, we drove away as the two small children stared at us through the window. We slowly made our way up a large mountain, then headed straight down a steep, winding, narrow road with no guard rails, hugging the side of the mountain. It overlooked a large green valley, and although the driving was scary, it definitely added to the adventure. We drove for another half hour before reaching a paved road, then headed along the mountainous coast to Jaco Beach.

"Dawn, look. It's the ocean."

As we drove over the mountain, we could see the Pacific off in the distance. Dawn looked so excited.

We arrived at the Jaco Beach Hotel in the evening. It was situated near the ocean in a tropical setting with palm trees and other exotic vegetation. We could hear birds and parrots as they flew by, and the sound of the ocean in the background. We checked in and carried our boards and suitcases to our room. It was a small room with tiled floors and a double bed in the center, located on the south side of a u-shaped, three-story complex. We dropped off our bags, and quickly went outside.

It was too late for a surf session, but we walked to the beach anyway. We could hear the waves pounding in the distance.

As we got closer, I pointed to a huge wave that had just broken, and said, "Dawn, did you see that?"

She looked up and saw a thundering wall of white water, but didn't say a word. I wasn't sure how Dawn would handle the power and size of the waves, but I knew she would be determined.

We went to bed early, and the next morning woke up just before sunrise. The Costa Ricans do not recognize daylight savings time, so in April the sun rises about five o'clock. I popped out of bed, ran to the window and cracked open the shade.

"Dawn wake up! The sun is just about ready to rise."

She looked tired, but jumped out of bed anyway, and said, "Let's go."

We threw on our bathing suits, put on our sunglasses and sandals, grabbed the surfboard wax off the dresser, and headed out the door. It was warm and humid when we stepped outside, and the unfamiliar sounds of birds squawking and iguanas scurrying to safety added to our excitement. We looked toward the ocean and saw large glassy waves peeling off in perfection, then quickly loaded our boards into the back of the pickup, and took off. Our plan was to surf at Hermosa Beach, a popular surf-break several miles south of Jaco, known for it's big powerful waves. We decided to stop at one of my favorite bakeries to pick up some fresh baked bread before our road trip. It was located on a back street in a little twelve by twelve concrete building with only one window and a door in front.

I walked in with Dawn and said, "Hola."

A young man with a white apron was pulling several freshly baked loaves of bread out of a small oven. He looked up at me and nodded his head while placing the steaming hot loaves on the counter.

"I'll take one of those," I said.

The baker obviously didn't speak much English so I pointed to one of the loaves on the counter.

"Si," he said, nodding his head.

After placing two large containers of fresh orange juice on the counter, Dawn pointed to some freshly baked pastries behind the glass. Surprisingly, our breakfast cost less than four hundred colonies, just a little over two dollars American.

We paid the baker and left right away. I wanted to get to the beach as early as possible. In the morning an off shore breeze is prevalent, making the waves glassy with perfect form. As we drove along the cliffs on our way to Hermosa Beach, we could see a huge ground swell below as the waves from the Pacific pounded against the rocks. The views were breathtaking. We

View from the cliffs on the way to Hermosa Beach

stopped on the shoulder of the road for a moment and looked down at the waves as they peeled off. Costa Rica was truly a surfers paradise.

We came down off the mountain and arrived at a farm gate that blocked the entrance to Hermosa Beach. To get to most of the popular surf spots in Costa Rica, you had to travel through privately owned farmland and, fortunately, the farmers did not seem to mind.

Entrance gate to Hermosa Beach

The gates were there not to stop people from coming in, but to keep the live stock from leaving. As usual, there were several small Tico children waiting to open the gate. As we went through, Dawn handed them some quarters and surf stickers. We rode down a bumpy dirt road and parked under the famous tree at Hermosa and looked at the ocean. For the first time, we saw the full size and shape of the waves. They were much larger

The famous tree at Hermosa

75

and more powerful than we had ever anticipated, at least six to eight feet, with up to fifteen-foot faces, and there was hardly anyone out.

Dawn and I were really excited. We got our boards out of the pickup as quickly as possible and made our way to the beach. The beach seemed abandoned, except for several dogs running off in the distance. Civilization, the way we knew it, did not exist. I can still feel that black sand between my toes. The black beaches in Costa Rica were created by years and years of volcanic activity. I looked at Dawn as she kneeled down in the sand waxing her surfboard. Neither one of us said a word, but the expression on her face said it all. She loved the unknown and, most of all, the adventure of it.

We had both trained for months on end for the hard paddle out, lifting weights and spending hours paddling through the surf. Even when there were no waves, we would paddle against the strong outgoing tide at the Sebastian Inlet. I believe that the anticipation of the trip and training with Dawn was half the fun.

Now we were ready. The sun had just come up and the waves were perfect. Our plan was to find a good rip current that would help carry us out. We found a good spot and jumped in together. I paddled as hard as I could, then, with perfect timing, I was able to duck dive under a large set-wave, a technique used to escape being pounded by large waves by diving underneath with your surfboard. Luckily I made it past the heavy shore break without incident. As soon as I felt it was safe, I stopped paddling and turned around on my board, hoping to see Dawn right behind me, but she was not as fortunate. She got hit so hard by a large wave that it blasted her fifty feet backwards nearly to the beach, pulling her bathing suit down below her knees. After she gained her composure, Dawn had a look of sheer determination on her face. She struggled for about ten minutes, jockeying through the waves and white water, and finally made it out. I didn't realize how tough Dawn was until that day. She was exhausted, but never gave up.

"Are you all right?" I asked.

"Yeah, I'm Ok," she responded, annoyed with herself.

I began the surf session by taking off on smaller waves. My intention was to get the feel of the swell. After catching several waves, I noticed that Dawn hadn't caught one yet and seemed upset with herself. I duck dove through a large wave and when I came up, Dawn was paddling toward a really giant one, looking obsessed. I didn't say anything, but deep down inside I was hoping she wouldn't take off on that wave, although I knew better.

Dawn confirmed my suspicions - she went for it. The wave had to be eight to ten feet with about a sixteen-foot face. This was definitely the wave of the day. She lined herself up with the highest peak and started paddling. To me, she appeared to be too deep inside and the wave looked like it was ready to collapse on her. I could feel her intensity as she paddled with everything she had. Every muscle of her five-foot-two-inch frame was in motion. Just as I began to duck dive through the monster wave, I saw Dawn at the point of no return. She loved it! Dawn took off without hesitation and dropped straight down the face of the wave.

"Hoo - hoooo!!!" She yelled in excitement.

At the bottom of the wave, she turned her board hard to the right. The wave was so big and powerful that it sounded like a freight train barreling behind her.

"Woooof!"

The giant wave collapsed, spraying the back of her neck.

When I came up on the other side of the wave, I quickly scanned the area, hoping that I would see her safely pop up to the surface. After about six seconds, I heard Dawn whistling in excitement. I made eye contact with her and she gave me the hang loose sign, a hand signal used to express appreciation of something good. She actually made it, and from that moment on, I realized that someone had to be watching over her - it couldn't have been all determination. Dawn paddled back out full of excitement. She was grinning from ear to ear.

"Did you see my wave?"

"Not all of it. Did you get a good ride?"

"It was great," she answered. "I hit the lip of the wave three times. Could you see the spray?"

"No, I couldn't. I saw you take off, then you disappeared behind it. It was huge."

After riding that monster wave, Dawn's confidence was high and she began catching wave after wave - she was fearless. After we were totally exhausted, we paddled to shore. The locals stared at Dawn in wonder. She was definitely something special, and fortunately for me, she was mine.

Costa Rica was a country where Dawn could test her physical limitations. After we loaded our boards onto the pickup for our trip back to the hotel, she decided to do something crazy. Dawn had a fascination and love for all animals, and about fifty yards away from our truck was a Brahma bull. Dawn had been curious about the huge bull all day, and wanted to get a closer look - I knew she couldn't pass up the opportunity. She slowly snuck up behind the bull, trying to pat its rump.

Dawn trying to catch a pig

I shouted to her, "What the hell are you doing?" but there was no response. When she made her mind up to do something, there wasn't a man on earth who could stop her. She got about fifteen feet from the bull, when he grunted and turned abruptly toward her.

I yelled again, "Get out of there! Your gonna get hurt."

I shook my head in disgust.

"She won't listen," I thought.

The bull took one look at Dawn, put his head down and, with his huge horns, charged at her.

"Oh shit!" she shouted.

Dawn sprinted in circles with the huge bull close behind.

The Brahma bull that chased Dawn

After several minutes, she managed to dive for safety under a nearby fence, rolling in the tall grass, and laughing with excitement. Then, when I got close enough with the truck, she sprinted toward me.

Holding the steering wheel with one hand, I reached over, opened the passenger door, and shouted, "Jump in!"

She dove into the pickup head first. I quickly grabbed onto

the back of her bathing suit so she wouldn't fall out, and drove off. The bull was really in a rage, and I thought for sure he was going to ram us. We finally got by him by speeding through a bumpy grass field.

"Are you all right?"

She sat up, nodded her head and started laughing.

"That bull could have killed you."

"I know, but it wasn't fast enough."

We both laughed, while I shook my head in disbelief.

That night at one of the local restaurants, we celebrated our first day with beer and fresh sea bass. We enjoyed eating and listening to the locals as they told their surf stories. It was obvious that Dawn could fit in anywhere.

We would wake up every morning around five and head to the local bakery. After eating our fresh baked bread and pastries, we would choose a good surf spot and surf for several hours. When we finished, it was time for lunch. You had to eat before noon in Costa Rica, because after that it was siesta time. Siesta meant that everyone was sleeping. This was my favorite time of day. After our nap, Dawn and I would head out for another session, and surf until we couldn't see the mountains in the distance.

I remember one evening sitting on my surfboard next to Dawn, watching the sun melt into the Pacific.

"It's so beautiful," she said. "Wouldn't you like to live here?"

"Maybe someday after we retire," I said. "It's so laid back and peaceful."

It was getting dark, so we both caught the next wave and rode it all the way to shore. By the end of our surf session, we were both famished and exhausted, a healthy kind of exhaustion from exercising in the fresh air all day. After supper, a few beers, and swapping war stories with the locals, we collapsed in bed.

As the week went by, we became close friends with many of

Bill and Dawn with their Costa Rican friends

the locals. Dawn and I enjoyed their innocence and sincerity. Costa Ricans are a proud people, who flourish in a very simple life style - no commercialism. They enjoy life and appreciate the beauty and natural aspects of their land.

In a conversation one day with one of the Costa Ricans, he happened to mention a waterfall that was south of Jaco Beach.

"It's spectacular," he said. "My friends and I go swimming there quite often,"

"Is it a large fall?" I asked.

"It's about five hundred feet high, hidden in a rain forest with pools of cold water that you can jump into."

We were so intrigued that we agreed to skip a siesta in search of the falls. I thought of a close friend of mine, Peko, a Tico Indian who I knew would give us directions. He was a guide and surfer in his middle twenties. He knew every interesting spot in Costa Rica, and on several previous surf trips, I used him as my personal guide. He would take me to unfamiliar surf spots, natural rain forests and active volcanos that were magnificent.

I went to the hotel manager and asked if he had seen Peko. He told me that Peko lived in a small, single-axle trailer that was parked in a vacant field just north of the hotel. We walked about four hundred yards along the beach just north of the hotel, and found it hidden amongst some overgrown shrubs and palm trees. It was an old, unkempt, tan and white trailer in dire need of a pressure cleaning. We apprehensively walked up to the door. It appeared as if no one was home. I knocked on the door, but no one answered.

"He's probably sleeping," Dawn whispered.

"It's one thirty. He should be up by now."

I knocked a little harder.

"What do you want?" someone said in a tired voice.

"I'm looking for Peko," I answered. "Do you know where he is?"

I could hear someone shuffling around inside.

"Bill, is that you?"

Peko appeared at the door. We shook hands and embraced.

"This is my wife, Dawn."

He gave her the once over, then gave me the hang loose sign.

"Are you still guiding surf trips?" I asked.

"Occasionally, but I spend most of my time commercial fishing with my family. I'm usually gone for two and three months at a time."

"Do you still surf?" I asked.

"Sporadically. How long have you been in Jaco?"

"We've been here for a week and plan to leave in a couple of days."

"It's nice to see you again. Do you need me to guide for you?"

"No. We're trying to find a waterfall about an hour south of here, and I was hoping you could give us directions."

"Sure, but I would be glad to take you."

"Great! We'll pick you up about eleven o'clock tomorrow morning after our surf session," I said.

"Would you mind if I brought a friend?" Peko asked.

"Not at all."

We shook hands again and left, so he could finish his afternoon nap.

We were still in our bathing suits when we picked up Peko and his companion the next day. His friend turned out to be his cousin, who lived with him in between fishing trips. They were dressed in t-shirts and shorts and just as anxious as we were to get to the falls. We headed south along the coast on the paved road from Jaco, and drove for a half hour, before turning down a dirt road through the middle of a date-palm field. There were large date-palm orchards all along the coast with acres and acres of palms, lined up in rows. We drove through the orchard for several miles before it ended, then continued on through a tropical rain forest, leading to the mountains in the distance. You could actually see and hear families of howler monkeys as they made their way through the jungle. Although they were small, the protective males sounded like gorillas. Traveling up a narrow, bumpy, dirt road, we also heard toucans and parrots squawking as they flew over head. Dawn and I felt like we were in a tropical paradise.

We stopped at a small hut nestled in the jungle, parked our truck, and hiked about two miles on a narrow, winding path through the jungle. The vegetation was so thick that it partially blocked the sun light. Finally, we made it to a clearing and saw the exotic waterfall for the first time. It was magnificent, situated right in the middle of a plush green forest. The waterfall was layered resembling giant steps, as the sparkling water descended from the top of the mountain. At the bottom of each step was a small pool of crystal-clear water. As we approached the falls, we saw some Costa Ricans jumping off a twenty-foot cliff into a small, circular, deep pool, which was surrounded by shallow

Dawn and Bill walking down a dirt road in Costa Rica

rocks and boulders. We watched as the locals climbed gingerly, scaling the rocks to an overhang. They would stop on a small platform and then slowly work their way to the edge, where they jumped in feet first.

"We've got to try it," Dawn said.

"Are you sure you want to?"

What a dumb question. Dawn had already taken off running toward the falls.

I sprinted past her and said, "I'm going first!"

I crossed the river, jumping from one rock to another, trying to get to the narrow path that led to the falls. When my feet touched the water, it was much colder than I anticipated. I climbed up the rock wall slowly inching my way to the top. There wasn't a cloud in the sky, and the temperature was in the lower eighties, although the shade made it feel much cooler. I carefully worked my way to the edge, then apprehensively looked down at Dawn, took a deep breath, and made the plunge.

I hit the water with a giant splash. It was definitely a thrill ride worth remembering.

Now it was Dawn's turn. She climbed to the top with about six of us watching her. I don't think the Costa Ricans were used to women being so physically active and fearless. Even Peko and his friend stopped and watched. She got to the top and decided to do something different. She climbed out onto a small limb about four inches in diameter that jutted out over the center of the small pool. Dawn worked her way out, balancing herself with her arms straight out from her side as if she were on a tight rope. She made it out about eight feet from the rock wall and stopped. She looked down at me and smiled.

"Don't! You'll kill yourself!" I shouted.

She did a front flip into the pool and over rotated slightly. I thought for sure that she hit her head on the surrounding rocks. Everyone looked amazed. Dawn was definitely a thrill seeker. I looked into the pool hoping that she hadn't broken her neck, and then suddenly she popped to the surface. At first it pissed me off, but when I saw her smile, I just gave a long sigh of relief.

The next day we packed our bags, threw the surfboards into the back of the pickup and headed to the airport. We were both totally relaxed and it seemed hard to believe our honeymoon was over. We arrived in San Jose and returned the pickup covered with mud, unloaded our boards and suitcases, then hustled to the Lasca Airlines check-in counter. After handing in our luggage, we quickly went to our departure gate and collapsed on a vacant bench next to each other. Dawn put her feet up on the bench and rested her head on my lap as I sunk back, leaning heavily against a wall. The trip had definitely taken much more out of us than either one of us had anticipated. I looked at Dawn as she slowly drifted off to sleep. She was oblivious to the noise around us, and looked so peaceful as I listened to her breathe.

Several minutes passed... I had just nodded off when I was wakened by, "Lasca Airlines flight number 647 will be boarding in five minutes..." in Spanish.

"Dawn... Wake up. It must be time to go."

She looked at me and said, "Ok."

We handed in our boarding passes, walked onto the plane, found our seats, fastened our safety belts, and drifted off to sleep within minutes after taking off. By the time we arrived at the airport in Miami, it was nine pm. We went to the baggage claim area, gathered our belongings as quickly as possible, found our pickup, and headed north on I-95. We were both totally exhausted and after only an hour, I had to pull off onto the shoulder of the road.

"Dawn, would you mind driving? I'm having trouble keeping my eyes open."

"Sure," she said.

She lasted about forty-five minutes, then I had to take over again. Finally, after three and a half hours, we made it home.

Chapter 8

The next morning I woke up still groggy from our honeymoon. Dawn had on her red, two-piece, lifeguard bathing suit and had already filled her duffel bag with sun block, running shoes, a towel, and an extra change of clothes. She was ready to start her rigorous training routine. We sat down at our breakfast table for the first time in ten days, and had cereal and milk with fruit on top. It felt great to be home, but neither one of us was anxious to go back to work.

"Are you going to enter any lifeguard competitions this year?" Dawn asked.

"I'm not sure," I answered.

"You could win in beach flags. You're a natural runner."

"What division would I compete in?" I asked.

"...Let me see. You'll be thirty-nine in December," she said, thinking out loud. "You'll have to compete in the twenty-nine to thirty-eight age division."

"Great!" I replied sarcastically.

"Don't worry. You can do it."

Dawn felt confident that if we both trained hard, we could medal, but she knew the competition would be keen.

Most lifeguard agencies are very competitive, and consider training and competition an important element of the job. Practicing is a large part of a lifeguards duty, enabling them to hone in on their own physical abilities and lifesaving skills. To perform a rescue in hazardous conditions takes both strength and stamina. Regularly scheduled physical testing is a common practice within most local agencies, and is utilized to assess ones own abilities against the standards that are set by similarly trained guards.

Every summer, starting in June, the United States Lifesaving Association (USLA), an organization recognized throughout the world as a benchmark in the lifeguard profession, sponsors regional and national competitions. The rivalry among the competing agencies is fierce, pushing the current standards to new levels.

The USLA has divided the country into geographical regions, with Vero Beach being part of the Central region, which includes Georgia, South Carolina and the Bahamas. The regional competitions are first, followed by the National Lifeguard Championship usually held in July, considered by the guards as the most prestigious lifeguard competition in the country. Each year the competition is held at a different location, changing the conditions from the warm ocean waters of Florida and Hawaii to possibly the cold waters of Lake Michigan. Registered lifeguard competitors from all over the country flock to the competition to challenge other contestants. The events consist of swimming, rowing, paddle board, running, sprinting and other team lifesaving events.

On the regional level, Dawn would compete in several different events, *The Two Mile Run, Paddle Board, Run-Swim-Run, Iron Woman,* and her favorite event, *Beach Flags.* Beach Flags is a sprinting contest that takes place on the beach. Competitors line up stomach down in the sand with their chins resting on their overlapped hands, facing in the direction opposite flags that are stuck in the sand. The flags are made of straight, half-inch, hard-rubber hose, cut into twelve inch sections with no flag attached. There is one less flag than the number of competitors (single elimination). When the whistle blows, the competitors turn and sprint thirty yards toward the flags, then dive in an attempt to capture one. The winner is the lifeguard who captures the last flag.

Two years before we were married, Dawn won a gold medal

in beach flags at Daytona Beach, Florida, at the Regionals, and a Gold medal in the National Lifeguard Championship in Pompano Beach, Florida. Unfortunately, the following year, she broke her gold medal streak at the National Championships in Chicago, Illinois, by finishing second and capturing a silver. Upset by her loss, Dawn badly wanted to win another gold and a second National Lifeguard Championship in Galveston, Texas.

We had just three months to train for our first competition, so we started right away. During my twenty-four hour shift at work, I would lift weights for two hours, followed by a thirty minute run, and then run wind-sprints in the parking lot behind the station, until my legs burned.

Dawn thought I had a lot of potential, and, on my days off, began teaching me all of her strategies and training techniques. It was mostly hard work. We would start by stretching for fifteen minutes, followed by a slow twenty minute jog on the beach to warm up. After relaxing for a couple of minutes and drinking lots of water, we would begin practicing beach flags in the deep sand. We would start by striking a line in the sand with our feet, then pace off thirty yards and make another mark. We would line up side by side with our stomachs in the sand, in the opposite direction from the thirty yard mark.

When we were both set in the ready position, Dawn said the starting words, "Heads up, heads down."

We would both jump to our feet while turning toward the marker, simulating the actual event, and sprint as hard as we could to the finish line.

After losing several races on the first day of training, I said to Dawn, "To make it fair, we should each take a turn saying the starting words."

"Why?" she asked.

"By the time you say "heads down,' you're already on your feet running,"

After I argued my case for several minutes, she agreed. We

raced for another fifteen minutes and by the time we finished, we were dead even. Dawn was a powerful runner with the muscular legs of a sprinter, a great competitor, and loved being challenged by me.

After Dawn got home from work, we would both prepare dinner, sit down and eat a big healthy meal filled with lots of carbohydrates. After dinner, if we weren't too tired, we would head back out to the gym and lift weights. This was our lifestyle for months on end. Looking back on it, we definitely pushed each other beyond our normal limits.

After months of training, Dawn thought I was ready for my first test as a competitor, so she signed me up for the East Coast Regional Championships in Jacksonville, Florida. On the day of the competition, we woke up before sunrise, drove over two and a half hours north to the Jacksonville city limits and headed east, following signs for the beach. The competition took place at the Mayport Naval Base, a small military installation located right on the Atlantic Ocean. We pulled into a large parking lot, grabbed our duffel bags, and walked through a vacant area filled

Dawn and Bill after their Regional competition

with saw-grass and other native vegetation. The beach was fenced off for military use only and was over a hundred yards wide. It had fine, white-powdered sand and bleachers set up, so the competitors could sit and relax between events. The beach was nearly deserted, except for several competitors walking in the distance, checking out the conditions. We walked down to the waters edge. The morning air felt cool, but there wasn't a cloud in the sky and it was obviously the start of a hot day. We looked out into the ocean. There was a ten mile an hour breeze coming directly off the water, making the seas two to three feet.

"It's choppy," Dawn said. "It's going to be a tough day for water events."

We had both signed up for the two mile run and knowing that it was typically the first event of the day, I asked Dawn, "Are you wearing your running shoes?"

Looking down at the wet sand, she said, "I think we should. The beach is hard packed, and I don't want to hurt my feet before beach flags."

Running barefoot on the beach can be very hard on your legs and feet, and if the sand is hard packed, it's much easier if you wear running shoes.

Someone blew a whistle, Beep, beep, beep.

We looked toward the bleachers and noticed a large man in a gray lifeguard referee shirt and a big straw hat, trying to get everyone's attention.

As we walked up, he said, "Everyone take a seat..."

The crowd of contestants slowly gathered.

"Does anyone need a schedule?" he asked.

No one responded.

"The first event of the day is the two mile run. We will start at the cones set up in front of the bleachers."

The cones were over fifty yards away, near the water's edge.

"There is another cone that you can't see that is just beyond the jetty."

He pointed to a row of boulders that were partially buried in the sand several hundred yards south of the bleachers.

"When the whistle blows, start running south. There will be a red jeep a hundred yards in front of you as your guide, so follow it."

He pointed to a jeep parked at the south end of the bleachers, with a black roll bar and no top.

"The race will start at exactly nine o'clock... Any questions?" he asked.

No one had any.

"I'll see you in ten minutes at the starting line."

Everyone got down off the bleachers and started getting prepared. Dawn and I put on our running shoes, and started stretching, trying to loosen our legs.

"Everyone line up," the official yelled.

"Good luck," I said to Dawn.

She slapped me five. Over a hundred competitors rushed to the starting line. Everyone was huddled together in one massive group, jockeying for position. Dawn and I somehow worked our way to the front of the crowd, then got into the ready position. Our knees were bent with one foot in front of the other, our arms swaying back and forth in anticipation of the whistle.

"On your mark. Get Set." Beep!

Everyone took off at once, then from the middle of the pack, a short muscular guard sprinted twenty-five yards ahead. He's going out too fast, I thought to myself. But not wanting to fall too far behind, I started running faster than my normal pace. For the first three hundred yards, I positioned myself near the front along with twelve other runners, and after another two hundred yards, 'the rabbit' was quickly overtaken and absorbed into the pack. The sun was getting warmer and the pace was much faster then I had anticipated. We followed the jeep over the jetty, then watched it stop at the halfway marker. One of the officials in the jeep stood up and waved us around. I ran around

the halfway marker still in the lead group, and felt pretty strong
as we started back toward the finish line. I saw Dawn for the first
time. She was not far behind, and gave me a thumbs up as she
passed by. With only several hundred yards left, my legs started
to tire and I quickly fell off the lead pace. Several runners passed
me so I tried to push harder, but I had totally run out of steam.
By the time I crossed the finish line, I had fallen out of the lead
pack and out of medal contention. Feeling nauseous, I bent over
with my hands on my knees, trying to catch my breath. When I
lifted my head, I happened to see Dawn sprint across the finish
line.

After recuperating, I walked over to Dawn and said, "Good
race."

"How did you do?" she asked inquisitively.

"Better then I expected. But not good enough for a medal."

"How do you think I did?"

"I only saw one woman ahead of you. I'm sure you
medaled."

We both walked to the bleachers, sweating profusely,
grabbed two water bottles and oranges peels off a table, and sat
down to rest.

After reviewing my schedule, I saw that beach flags was the
last event of the day, so I had plenty of time to recover. Dawn,
however, had a rigorous day ahead. Her next event started in
twenty minutes. It was the *Run-Swim-Run*, an event that started
with a two hundred yard beach run, followed by a four hundred
yard ocean swim, and ending with another two hundred yard
run to the finish line.

Dawn took off her running shoes and laid down on the
bleachers, trying to relax. The whistle blew, signaling it was time
for her race. We walked down to the waters edge.

"Are you ready?" I asked.

"I think so," she replied.

"Good luck."

She looked determined, but was apprehensive, knowing this was not her strongest event. Dawn lined up in the front of the pack. She had her swim cap on, and was wearing a red lifeguard bathing suit. The whistle blew and she sprinted the first two hundred yards, beating everyone into the water. She swam as fast as she could, but was overtaken as she rounded the buoy at the halfway mark. When she reached the beach, she had five contestants ahead of her. She gained some ground by sprinting past two competitors, but only managed to finish fourth, just out of medal contention. Dawn was disappointed, but she gave it her all.

Her next event was the thousand yard paddle board race, an event where competitors line up on the beach with their paddle boards, a twelve foot foam board coated with fiberglass, used to rescue bathers in distress. When the whistle blows, the competitors run into the water, jump on their boards, kneeling or lying, and paddle for five hundred yards around a buoy marker and then back. The race ends after they paddle to shore and carry their boards across the finish line.

In previous years, she would enter the race for the fun it, but not now. After learning how to surf and practicing hard all year for the event, she felt strong. Dawn lined up alongside the other competitors with her paddle board in hand. She was ready. The whistle blew. She ran into the water, dragging her board behind until she was about knee deep, then jumped on her board and paddled as hard as she could through the powerful shore break. After she passed the impact zone, she popped up into the kneeling position, and started thrusting back and forth paddling with everything she had.

"Come on, Dawn, you can do it," I shouted excitedly.

She looked like a machine. On each stroke, she reached forward putting both arms into the water at the same time and pulled as hard as she could, propelling her board forward through the water. She rounded the first buoy in the front of the pack, and paddled toward another buoy off in the distance. Then, because of the rough seas, I lost sight of her about three hundred yards out. Shortly after, I noticed a tight group of competitors round the halfway marker. I hoped that Dawn was still in front, but couldn't be sure. As they paddled closer, I saw her side by side with two other female competitors.

"Paddle hard!" I yelled.

She rounded the last buoy in second place with only a hundred yards to go. Dawn gave it her all and managed to catch a wave about halfway to shore. She rode the wave past her competition, jumped to her feet, grabbed the handle on the side of her board, and dragged it across the finish line, capturing the gold. She threw her board down and jumped for joy.

"All right!" I yelled. "You did it."

I ran up to her and she jumped into my arms.

"Did you see me ride that wave?"

"It was perfect," I said.

We walked up to the bleachers and Dawn collapsed. She had one more event left before beach flags and, fortunately, it didn't start until after lunch. It was the iron woman event, a combination of three races in one, starting out with a four hundred yard beach run, followed by a four hundred yard swim, and ending with a four hundred yard paddle board race to the finish line. After her gold medal in the paddle board, Dawn's confidence was high.

The race started out with no surprises. After the run, she was first into the water. She was overtaken in the swim, but stayed close enough to the lead to be in contention. After she jumped on her paddle board, she quickly gained some ground on the lead pack. About halfway through the race she passed the sixth place competitor, then, just before the last buoy, she paddled passed the fifth and fourth place competitors. When she rounded the last buoy on the home stretch, she zoomed past the third place competitor and captured the bronze. This was her first time ever competing in the iron woman event, and it was evident to everyone that she was quickly becoming a dominant force in the lifeguard profession.

Beach flags was next, the last event of the day. It took place in front of a sports bar, a hundred yards west of the bleachers. It was designed so that competitors would start the race on the east side of the sand pit, facing the ocean, and would end with them diving for flags in front of the crowd.

The women's division was first. There were tables and seats everywhere, with over a hundred spectators. Dawn walked into the pit full of confidence and determination. She was one solid muscle, and highly favored to win.

"You can do it, Dawn," I yelled.

The crowd started hooting and hollering in anticipation of the start.

The whistle blew, Dawn jumped to her feet while turning, sprinted, then dove through the air capturing a flag. She made it look easy and everyone cheered and clapped at her victory. She lined up again, but now there was one less flag and competitor than the first race. The whistle blew, and again she dove for a flag with ease. Dawn won round after round, and for her third year in a row, she captured the gold medal at the regional's.

"Great job," I said, while passing her on my way into the pit.

"Now it's your turn," she responded.

I walked up to the starting line with the jitters. Being thirty-eight years old and competing against lifeguards who were twenty-nine made me nervous. I wasn't sure of my chances, but it was Dawn's faith in my abilities that kept me motivated. I stretched my legs while the lifeguard official gave us his final instructions.

I lined myself up on the outside of the pack. There were six of us. Everyone became silent. I got myself situated in the sand, and tried to remember everything Dawn had taught me.

United States Lifeguard Association Regional competition -
Jacksonville, Florida

The official said the starting words, "Head up, heads down."

Beep! I jumped to my feet and turned at the same time, then keeping as low to the ground as possible, I pushed off in the sand and sprinted toward the flags as hard as I could. Five yards from the flag, I dove for it.

I stood up with the flag in my hand, and heard Dawn yell, "All right!"

Confident, I walked back to the starting line and got positioned in the sand again. The whistle blew and, in perfect timing, I took off and captured a second flag. The crowd was clapping and cheering. Two more rounds passed and, somehow, I made it to the finals. I lay in the sand with my heart pounding in anticipation. There were just two of us left and only one flag. The whistle blew. I sprinted for the last flag using every ounce of energy I had. I don't know how close it was, but when I got up with that last flag in my hand, the only thing I could focus on was Dawn's smile.

"We did it!" I shouted.

We were both East Coast Regional Champions.

After the contest was over, the head official announced, "There will be an award ceremony in twenty minutes."

Everyone slowly walked to a stage set up outside the volleyball pit and grabbed a seat.

"I'd like to thank everyone for participating in today's events," the head official announced over the microphone. "It was a great turnout."

Everyone applauded.

"I'm going to start with the medal winners of the first event and work my way through the last event of the day. When you hear your name, please step up to the stage as quickly as possible and collect your medal."

After receiving three medals, Dawn stepped up to the stage to collect her gold medal in beach flags.

"Not you again," the head official said.

Everyone laughed. Then he announced the winners of my division. Walking to the stage to collect my gold medal, I was completely overwhelmed with joy and felt like a teenager again. We celebrated with our fellow competitors for hours that night, dancing and reminiscing about the days events. When we finally made it home, Dawn fell asleep in my arms. Dawn was not just my lover, she was my best friend.

Our next competition took place at the National Lifeguard Championships in Galveston, Texas. On my first day back at work after the regionals, I went straight to the chief's office and asked him for permission to attend the competition.

"Can you win?" he asked.

"I'm not sure, but you know I'll give it my best."

He leaned back in his chair.

"How much are the airline tickets?"

"Probably under three hundred dollars."

"I'll give you one shift off and pay for your ticket," he said generously. "The rest you'll have to deal with."

I left his office, called Dawn, and gave her the news. She was thrilled that we were both going.

We had one month to prepare, but decided to rest for several days before starting back on our rigorous exercise routine. On our first day of training, my muscles felt stiff and sore. The regional competition had taken much more out of me than I had expected. We trained day after day for three and a half weeks preparing for the nationals.

Finally it was time to leave. We took off from the Orlando airport in the morning and landed in Houston, Texas that afternoon. When we got off the plane, I thought we were still at home. The weather was hot and sticky with the sun shining brightly. We took a taxi to Galveston, a city situated on the Gulf of Mexico with huge pristine beaches. After unpacking our bags, we took a slow three mile run around the hotel area to loosen up. When we finished, we showered, got dressed and headed out to dinner. We ate in a small restaurant by the beach. After dinner, we searched for the tournament area and found it on the east end of Galveston. The beach was at least a quarter mile wide, extremely flat with white powdery sand, and a large two story building in the middle. The building had bathrooms and a concession stand inside, with banners hanging everywhere, advertising the competition. It was obviously going to be a major event.

Dawn and I took off our sandals, walked about a hundred yards in the deep sand and happened upon an area marked off with cones and ribbon.

"This must be the beach flag pit," I said.

An unknown beach flag competitor showed up to practice his starts, and after watching him for awhile, we couldn't resist and tried some ourselves. Then we caught a cab and headed back to our hotel room.

It was dark when we arrived and we were both exhausted, so we showered, and laid down in bed to watch television.

After only a half hour, Dawn said, "I'm tired. Let's go to

sleep. Besides, tomorrow is going to be a long day."

I agreed, and turned off the set knowing I would have trouble falling asleep. Entering a national event was a new experience for me and I felt anxious. Not Dawn, though. She was ready and knew all her toughest competitors by name. I remember looking over at Dawn as she slept, thinking how peaceful she looked. Dawn had nerves of steel, and when it came to competition, she knew what had to be done.

The next morning we woke up at six forty-five, got dressed, had breakfast, and headed directly to the beach. We wanted to get there early to check out the conditions. When we arrived, however, the beach was already packed with competitors milling around. We worked our way through the crowd and found two bulletin boards where all the scheduled events were posted.

"Beach flags doesn't start until three," I said. "When is your first event?"

Dawn had already begun scanning the other board.

"Paddle board. It starts at eleven," she replied.

Although we had three and a half hours to wait before her first competition, we decided to stay anyway. We walked to the ocean through groups of competitors stretching and warming up. The tide was going out and the water was murky from a two foot, wind chop. We stood in ankle deep water watching the men's *Run-Swim-Run* race. The slope on the beach was so gradual that the water stayed shallow for a long way out, making it difficult for us to see the competitors swimming off in the distance, but it was still fun for us watching world class athletes competing in their strongest events.

After watching for over a half hour, we walked to a concession stand and happened to run into a friend of Dawn's. He was a lifeguard from the county directly south of our hometown and was at the competition to compete in several team events.

"What are you competing in?" Dawn asked.

"The *Two-Man Dory*" (a wooden rowboat made for water res-cues) "and the *Team Line Pull* event" (a competition where a vic-tim was towed to shore, utilizing a rescue rope being pulled by two lifeguards on the beach), he said.

After Dawn told him she was competing in the thousand yard paddle board race, he asked, "Would you like to borrow one of our boards?"

We walked to where his team kept their equipment so Dawn could check out the board. It was a new model, twelve feet long, extremely light and streamlined, made for racing.

Dawn picked it up with one hand, and asked, "Are you sure no one else needs it?"

"I'm positive," he said.

"Thanks," she replied. "I'll return it as soon as I'm done."

We said good-bye and carried the board off so Dawn could practice. She had never tried a board specifically designed for racing before.

She walked down to the ocean and found a secluded area, pushed her board out until she was in knee deep water, then floated on top of it. At first, she appeared to have some difficul-ty balancing herself, but gradually she got the hang of it. After ten minutes of paddling around, she came to shore.

"Well, how did it feel?" I asked.

"Not bad, but it's different from any other board I've ever paddled on."

Our conversation was interrupted by someone on a mega-phone.

"The thousand yard women's paddle board race will start in five minutes."

We carried her board to the starting line as quickly as possi-ble. Dawn wasn't sure of her chances, but she certainly looked determined. She stood there in a crouched position, in the midst of twenty-five of the best women paddle boarders in the nation.

"All competitors ready," the official yelled, while pointing a small pistol in the air.

Bang! The gun sounded.

Dawn took off running, dragging her board into the water. She quickly paddled through the shore break and disappeared out of sight. As the race continued, the only thing I could see was an occasional glimpse of someone paddling off in the distance. Eighteen minutes later, I saw several small groups of paddle boarders racing to shore, but it was difficult to distinguish Dawn from the rest of the contestants. Finally, as they got closer, I was able to find her. She was at the rear of the front pack trying desperately to catch a large wave, but missed it while struggling awkwardly on her board. After gaining control, she rode the next wave to shore, but it was too late. She was out of medal contention.

"I lost sight of you right away. What happened?" I asked.

"I felt strong, but I couldn't get into a rhythm," she said.

Dawn was a very good sport and, although she was disappointed with her effort, she congratulated the winners.

We returned the board, thanked her friend, and decided to get some lunch. Dawn was not in the least bit discouraged about her race, and was already talking about next years strategy.

"I need to buy my own racing board before next season," she said. "It will make a big difference."

We walked on the sidewalk along the beach, passing every kind of souvenir shop imaginable. Every store was packed with competitors from all over the country, adding to the already festive atmosphere. After trying several restaurants, we were able to find a quaint spot with an open table. We sat down, ate our lunch, and continued to talk about all sorts of things. The time flew by so quickly that we almost forgot about the competition.

"It's quarter of three," Dawn said with a surprised look on her face. "We better hurry. Beach Flags starts at three."

We left the restaurant and rushed to the beach. Many of the

competitors had already begun to gather, and were anxiously waiting for the contest to begin.

"Anyone competing in the seniors division, ages twenty-nine through thirty-eight, report to the tent at the east end of the pit," the official announced over a megaphone.

I quickly said good-bye and hustled with the rest of the competitors to a twelve foot open tent. There were eighteen of us in all, varying in ages and physical stature.

The official called out our names individually,"... Schauman."

"Here," I replied.

After he called the last name, he said, "There will be several elimination rounds held this afternoon, with the remaining six competitors eligible for tomorrow's final round."

I made it through the first several rounds of competition without too much difficulty, and was able to advance to the final round of the day. When the referee called us to the starting line, I quickly maneuvered myself into an outside lane. There were seven of us left. I lay in the hot sand and concentrated, trying to anticipate the referee's words.

"Heads up, heads down". Bang! The gun sounded.

I jumped to my feet and sprinted toward the flag directly in front of me, with the two competitors right next to me apparently going for the same flag. I quickly scanned the other flags, and saw that there was one open flag available on the other side of them, but they were too preoccupied pushing and shoving each other to notice. Then in one giant leap, they both dove in front of me. I slowed down and crossed behind them, diving for the open flag. Unbelievably, I captured it, making it to the finals by the skin of my teeth. If it hadn't been for Dawn's advice on how to line up on the outside, I definitely would not have made it.

I ran to Dawn excitedly, and asked, "Did you see that finish?"

"Nice move," she responded, knowing how risky the maneuver was.

"All contestants who are signed up for the women's open, report to the officials' tent," a referee announced.

"You'd better hurry," I said.

She started walking toward the tent and I yelled, "Good luck!"

She turned and looked at me with a smile, then continued on her way.

The official took one look at the large group of competitors that had assembled in front of the tent and said, "Because there are so many of you, we'll be forced to hold preliminary rounds today and at the beginning of tomorrow's competition."

Dawn easily advanced to the next day's competition, winning almost every race by ten paces. She didn't even have to dive for the flag in some of her heats.

When the day was over, we were both famished and exhausted, but I felt uplifted, not expecting to make it to the finals. We ate right after Dawn's final race, caught a cab back to the hotel, and collapsed in bed. Unlike the first night, I fell asleep within minutes.

The next day we woke up late, stayed at the hotel until after lunch, then leisurely made our way to the beach, arriving a half hour before our competition. The beach flag pit was roped off so spectators would not interfere with the event. A large crowd was beginning to gather around the pit. It was hot and muggy, and the sun was intense, but it didn't bother me. Being in the finals in a national event was exhilarating, and my adrenaline was pumping.

"All senior division contestants report to the starting area," an official announced.

Six of us gathered around the official as he called out our names.

"Everyone's here, so line up," he said.

I positioned myself on the outside lane, waiting for the start. The gun sounded and I took off sprinting as hard as I could, then dove at the flag directly in front of me with everything I had, but it was not enough. My luck had finally run out, and I got knocked out in the first round. Although disappointed, I felt a sixth place in my age group wasn't anything to be ashamed of.

The women's open division was called to the starting line next. Dawn walked to the line with confidence. She wasn't cocky, but her muscular physique definitely intimidated her opponents.

"All contestants take your positions," the referee announced.

Dawn beating her competition easily

Dawn got situated in the sand. She looked obsessed. There was no way anyone was going to beat her. The gun sounded, and she sprinted past her competition, making it look easy. She continued to dominate every round, advancing to the finals with no difficulty.

Now it was judgement day - she was ready. I can still visualize the determination on her face. Dawn was lying on her stomach in the sand with her chin resting on her hands. She was thirty yards away, facing the opposite direction from the last

Bill and Dawn right after Dawn's victory in Galveston, Texas

Dawn wearing some of her lifeguard medals

beach flag. Next to her was a track star from William and Mary College, a member of the World Lifesaving Team. Dawn didn't talk about it much, but last year she beat Dawn in the finals on a controversial call. Now it was payback time - I could feel it.

The referee said the starting words, " heads up, heads down."

Bang! the gun went off.

I can see Dawn now - she looked like a machine charging through the sand with her muscular legs.

"Go, Dawn!" I yelled.

Then with one giant leap, she dove at the last beach flag. When the sand cleared, Dawn had the winning flag in her hand - she never looked so energetic and happy. When Dawn's happy, you can't help but smile with her.

Chapter 9

I couldn't stand it any more. I had to know what was going on in that operating room. Ten minutes had passed and I hadn't heard a thing. Somebody had to know something. I opened the door to the birthing room, peered out, and saw several nurses milling around the nurses station. I tried to get their attention, but they appeared to be avoiding me. My intuition told me that something was seriously wrong with Dawn, but I tried not to think of the worst.

Finally I couldn't wait any longer, so I walked to the nurses station and said, "Excuse me."

The nurse in charge, a stern, heavy-set woman, looked up at me and said, "Can I help you?"

"Yes. Have you seen the doctor or heard anything about Dawn's condition?"

The nurse hesitated, then said, "No, I haven't."

"Damn," I mumbled under my breath in frustration. "If you hear anything at all, please let me know."

"Of course," she said.

She knew I was upset, and in a compassionate and concerned voice, asked, "Do you need anything?"

" No thank you," I said anxiously, and went back into the birthing room. Once in the room by myself, I sat back down on the recliner and started thinking about all the possible consequences. I was completely overwhelmed and began praying out loud.

"Jesus, please forgive me."

" I know I haven't been a devoted Christian. Not even close!"

Then in desperation, I said, "I would sacrifice my own life to save Dawn's."

I truly believed that someone had to be watching over her.

Dawn was so pure in heart and spirit, it seemed impossible that she wasn't going to make it. She couldn't die and leave me and the kids. We had all been through so much together, and she knew how much we loved and needed her.

Dawn was a fighter, but that desperate look on her face as she passed out on the birthing room bed was still fresh in my mind.

I said to myself, as if she could hear me, "You and the baby will be Ok, Dawn."

"...You have to be Ok!!!"

The only thing that seemed to help was to focus on Dawn's spirit of life, and our adventures together. My thoughts drifted back in time again.

Chapter 10

Surfing with close friends is probably what the sport of surfing is all about. Catching a nice wave and having your best friends acknowledge the ride is something only a surfer can truly appreciate. It's not like hitting a home run or running for a touchdown, it's you alone with the ocean, trying to saddle Mother Nature's power. There's nothing more rewarding than to ride on a perfect wave, or more thrilling than to take off on a giant one and make the drop. The ocean is just so unpredictable. That's the attraction for me. I guess that must be one of the reasons that I am attracted to Dawn.

I recall one special experience when my brother Nick, Dawn, and I went surfing in front of the pavilion at Floridana Beach. This was the place where Dawn and I were married, our home town surf spot. When the waves were good and the weather was warm and sunny, it seemed like the whole neighborhood was out surfing. This particular New Year's Day was different. We picked Nick up in front of his house. He was already in his wetsuit, waiting with his board in hand, ready to go. We quickly loaded his board into the back and took off for the beach. The three of us were jammed in the front seat of my pickup, joking and kidding around in anticipation of surfing good waves. Nick reached over and cranked up the music on the radio. We pulled into the Floridana Beach parking lot, reserved for residents only, and came to a sudden stop by hitting the telephone pole that was lying across the grass, blocking any vehicles from entering. There was only one other pickup parked in the lot.

I threw the door open, and said enthusiastically, "James must be out!"

James was a friend of ours who loved to surf big glassy waves. We quickly got out, and Dawn and I put on our spring suits, a one-piece neoprene wetsuit with short sleeves that covers the torso down to the knees, designed to insulate the body in cool conditions.

"It's cold," Dawn said shivering, while struggling, pulling her skin tight wetsuit above her waist.

"Don't be a wimp," I responded sarcastically. "You'll be all right."

She playfully punched me in the arm.

As we pulled our boards out of the back of the pickup, Nick asked, "Who's got the wax?"

"I've got some," I replied. "Do you want it?"

"No, let's wax our boards on the beach," he said.

The three of us hurried over the dune crossover with our boards underarm.

"Look at those waves," Dawn said with a big smile on her face.

Looking out at the horizon, we could see a dense fog rolling in from the north, reminding me of a cool day on the New Jersey coast.

When we made our way down to the beach, we saw that James and another friend of ours were already surfing. We sat on the beach waxing our boards and watching the sets roll in. James caught a good wave on his long board, and paddled back out without any difficulty, indicating that there was no lateral current. We stretched in the sand for a few moments.

"Let's go!" I yelled after attaching my leash to my left ankle.

We all jumped in together and started paddling out. Although the water felt cool, no one complained, wanting to get started right away.

"Look at that left!" Nick shouted excitedly.

A giant wave was coming right at us. It's a unique experience when you're lying on your board looking up at a large wave barreling down on top of you. The three of us simultaneously duck dove our boards under the wave, then, after several seconds, popped to the surface and continued paddling past the impact zone. We paddled out about a quarter of a mile before meeting up with our friends.

"How are the waves?" I asked James.

"Not bad," he said while paddling on his stomach to catch one.

He took off and disappeared out of sight on a big right and reappeared several seconds later. The waves were a foot over head and glassy. The three of us joined in on the fun and began catching one wave after another. It was definitely turning out to be one of the better days of the winter season.

After catching a good wave, Dawn was paddling back out when she noticed something swimming about a hundred yards east of us in the mist.

"What's that?" she said to me inquisitively.

Peering through the fog, I saw a large flipper come out of the water.

"It's only a... manatee," I shouted.

Dawn wanted to get a better look, though, so she paddled toward it trying to follow the bubbles and turbulence coming up from below. I never thought she would actually get close enough to see what it was, but Dawn was determined and managed to get within ten feet of it. When it surfaced this time, I got a better look and couldn't believe my eyes. My heart was racing with excitement - it was incredible.

I yelled as loud as I could to Dawn, "It's a whale!"

She heard me and paddled furiously to keep up with it. We all watched as Dawn got closer and closer, until she was positioned directly over top of the whale. She leaned down to touch it when all of a sudden the water began to rumble. It sounded like a large submarine coming up from the deep. Then, out of nowhere, a giant mother whale, trying to protect her baby, broke the surface right behind Dawn, jumping completely out of the water.

"Dawn!" I shouted.

We could see the whole body of the whale. It was about sixty feet in length, with a huge head and giant tail. What a scary sight! I remember lying there on my board thinking about the movie, "Moby Dick." The only difference was that this was real. The mother whale came down with a giant splash.

Whoosh!!!

At first I was worried about Dawn, but then I laughed to myself when I saw her scramble to safety.

"What a nut!"

I've never seen Dawn paddle so fast. Her damn curiosity almost got her killed this time.

Chapter 11

It was mid October, and I had just called for a wave report for the Sebastian Inlet State Park. The park, located on Florida's east coast, is known for its surfing, fishing, shrimping, and camping.

"Thanks for calling the four o'clock wave report. It's mid-tide, and the surf is two to three feet and glassy," the recording said.

I hung up the phone and said,"All right!"

I immediately picked it back up and called Dawn.

"Tracking Station Park," she answered.

"Get your stuff ready," I said excitedly. "The inlet is going off" (surfer slang for great waves).

"I've just started closing up," she replied.

"I'll pick you up in fifteen minutes," I said.

"Bring something to eat."

"Ok!"

I hung up the phone, grabbed Dawn's favorite music cassettes off the kitchen counter along with a plastic container full of pasta, loaded my board in the pickup, and took off. When I drove into the Tracking Station parking lot, Dawn was already standing by the curb waiting, with her board and her duffel bag. She had changed into her one piece, french cut, bright purple bathing suit with yellow flowers, and looked anxious to go.

"What took you so long?" she asked, as she threw her stuff in the back.

"It's only been ten minutes," I said laughing. "Get in and stop complaining."

She jumped in and said, "Roll down the windows. It's

beautiful outside."

Dawn loved the fresh air. She put in one of her cassettes, turned up the volume, and we headed toward the inlet. It was perfect, not too hot, and no humidity. I slowed down as we crested the inlet bridge so we could get a better look at the waves. Monster Hole was classic, with huge glassy waves breaking on the outside. It's located on the south side of the inlet, and gets its nickname from the sharks that frequent the waters below. This famous break is known for its big waves and long paddle out.

"Look!" Dawn said.

There was a surfer on the north side of the inlet hitting the lip of a wave just before it broke, sending a magnificent spray of water into the air.

"Did you see that?" Dawn asked enthusiastically.

"Nice ride!" I replied. "The wind must be coming out of the southeast."

When the wind is blowing out of the south or southeast the north jetty acts like a barrier, making the surfing conditions on the north side ideal. The excellent surf conditions in the fall are created by unstable weather conditions. Low pressure systems push their way into the deep south, while hurricanes and tropical storms simultaneously develop off the coast of South Africa, with storm after storm spinning unpredictably across the Atlantic towards the east coast of the United States.

The only drawback to surfing at the Sebastian Inlet in autumn is the large amount of bait fish and sharks congregating at the jetty. The bait fish migrate south for the winter beginning in August, and by October they are at their peak. In the fall, you can actually watch the sharks and tarpon as they attempt to trap bait fish against the north jetty. It's like a wild roundup, with bait fish jumping and splashing everywhere. Even the pelicans and other birds dive bomb the water in an effort to capture an easy meal.

When we could no longer see the waves, I pushed down on the gas peddle, sped down the bridge, turned abruptly into the park entrance and quickly drove to the parking lot. Dawn and I jumped out of the pickup, grabbed our boards and quickly made our way over the wooden planks leading to the beach. We loved surfing in the evening, no heat, and a beautiful panoramic view of the sun setting. Wanting to avoid the crowds, we would normally surf several hundred yards north of the jetty, but today the parking lot was almost empty, and as we crossed the dune, we could see that there was hardly anyone out.

We waxed our boards and paddled out through the clear, warm water. A large wave broke in front of us and it felt refreshing to duck dive under it. We made it out past the breaking waves with ease, then sat on our boards with our feet dangling below the surface, waiting for some good ones to come. A few moments later a large set came through. Each of us caught a wave, then maneuvered back out.

"Fun waves," Dawn said.

"I had a great left," I replied. "I rode it all the way to the beach."

Another set rolled through and we both took off again. I rode down the face of the wave pumping my legs as hard as I could, maneuvering my board up and down the wave, then with perfect timing, I kicked my board out of the wave just before it collapsed.

"Hoo, hooo!" I yelled, while flying over the back side of the wave.

Uplifted from my ride, I paddled back out to Dawn. She was sitting about seventy-five yards north of the inlet, trying to catch the wedge off the jetty. The Sebastian Inlet has a concrete walkway extending about two hundred yards out into the ocean, supported with concrete pilings and large boulders that are stacked up underneath. When the waves come in and hit the jetty, they jack up several feet forming a wedge that is really fun to surf.

"How was your ride?" she asked.

"It was fun. I said.

Then it happened.

"Whoah!" I shouted.

Six feet in front of us we saw a large swirl in the water.

"It has to be a shark," I thought.

I didn't look over at Dawn, but I know we both picked up our feet at the same time. It's a normal reflex when you're surfing with bait fish and sharks. We looked for something to surface.

"It's big," I said to Dawn.

I knew it was down there somewhere - I could feel it. All of a sudden, a six foot spinner shark jumped out of the water, twisting in midair.

"Watch out, Dawn!" I shouted.

It landed less then ten feet from us.

"Did you see that?" We said at the same time.

It was scary, but we felt it was safe to be out as long as the water remained clear. Besides, the sharks weren't after us, they wanted their favorite meal of bait fish. The next wave was huge. We both paddled hard to catch it, but Dawn was in better position.

"Are you going?" I asked.

"What do you think!" she said sarcastically.

Reluctantly, I backed off. Dawn was just about ready to catch the wave... when she suddenly reared back and stopped. It caught me off guard.

"What's wrong?" I shouted.

"Not another shark," I thought to myself.

It wasn't. Right in front of Dawn was a swarming dark cloud of bait fish being chased by a large Tarpon. The frightened bait fish jumped across Dawn's surfboard in an attempt to escape. The Tarpon charged. With its mouth wide open and just six inches from Dawn's surfboard, it dove underwater nearly striking her on the leg. In my forty years of surfing, I had never seen anything quite like it.

"Dawn must have nine lives," I thought.

Frightened, she turned toward me, her eyes like big round saucers. We looked at each other without saying a word and paddled to shore.

Chapter 12

We had been married now for over a year. Dawn had always talked about having a big family. She wanted five. Maybe it was because she came from a large family, but really didn't understand the amount of work that was involved. Knowing Dawn could probably handle it, I agreed. She could make me agree to just about anything when she put her mind to it.

In May of 1993, we had just gotten back from another Costa Rican trip when Dawn found out she was pregnant. I was sitting in the kitchen having breakfast, when she ran out of the master bedroom holding a home pregnancy test in her hand. It looked like a thermometer with a small window on one end.

"I'm pregnant!" she said excitedly.

I looked at her, bewildered, knowing that we had just spent the past ten days surfing powerful waves in Costa Rica.

Ray, Steve, Bubba, Dawn, Bill, Nick, and Mike
on surf trip in Costa Rica

"Let me see," I said in shock, grabbing it out of her hand.

I had no idea what I was looking at.

"Do you see the solid red line?" she asked, while looking over my shoulder.

"Yes," I replied. "But it looks pink to me."

She quickly pulled out the directions and read them out loud.

"If nothing appears in the window, you are not pregnant... If a red line appears, you are pregnant," she read.

"I can't believe it. Why didn't you say something?" I asked.

"I guess I did feel nauseous the last couple of mornings in Costa Rica... But I didn't want to get your hopes up."

I grabbed her and squeezed her tightly. Her eyes filled with tears.

"Besides, you would've badgered me about surfing," she said.

"Well, you're going to have to take it easy," I replied.

"See, I knew it. You're already starting."

The next day, Dawn went to the doctors office to get a blood test. Although her hopes were high, she wanted to be sure.

"When can I get the results?" Dawn asked the nurse.

"Sometime this afternoon," she replied. "Call after four."

Dawn called the office later that day and it was confirmed. She hung up the phone and instantly called me at work.

"Indian River Shores Public Safety," an officer answered.

"Could I speak to Bill? It's important," She asked.

I picked up the phone, and answered, "Lieutenant Schauman."

"I got the test results and..."

"Are you pregnant?" I asked, not giving her time to finish.

"It came back positive," she said.

We were thrilled, and the next day we celebrated by going out to dinner.

At the beginning of her pregnancy, Dawn was still able to continue surfing and working out, so our life style didn't change very much. She never smoked, drank caffeine, or drank much alcohol, making it easy for her to maintain a healthy pregnancy. We always felt that by being active parents, our baby would be healthy and strong.

Of the two of us, I was the worrier. On my first visit to the obstetrician with Dawn, I questioned her doctor, a tall, slender, mild-mannered man in his early forties, about her condition.

"Can she surf?" I asked.

"Probably through the first trimester, but it depends on how she feels," he replied. "She's not sick, she's pregnant."

"How about lifting weights?" I asked.

"As long as she doesn't overdo it," he said.

Dawn had a told-you-so look on her face, and said, "Don't worry, I'm not going to do anything crazy."

Although Dawn was fearless, I knew, deep down, she would never do anything intentionally to harm our baby.

As the months passed, we finally reached the end of the first trimester. Dawn's doctor began to modify some of her activities, but said she was still able to surf. I thought the doctor and Dawn were both out of their minds. She wasn't going to quit surfing until she absolutely couldn't tolerate the discomfort any longer.

Then one day she came home from work very upset.

"What's wrong?" I asked.

She reluctantly answered, "When I went surfing at lunch... It just didn't feel right."

"Did you hurt yourself?"

She hesitated.

"I'll be all right."

Dejected, Dawn turned and walked away. I knew she was upset and when I asked her again, she turned and told me what happened.

"The pressure on my stomach from lying on my surfboard made me feel uncomfortable."

I tried to be sympathetic, but deep down inside I was hoping it was finally time for her to quit.

"It's your decision," I said.

Disappointed, she said, "I would never let anything happen to our child. I hope you understand that."

Holding her in my arms I said, "Of course I do."

Reluctantly, she gave up surfing that day. Her active life style was quickly coming to an end. Next it was basketball. She gave it up when she was four months pregnant.

At first, Dawn's lifeguard job was not much of a concern. She could still swim, lift weights, and perform her full work schedule and beach assignments. She hated the thought of being out of shape, but four and a half months into her pregnancy, she could no longer fit into her regular bathing suit, and was forced to wear a one piece maternity suit. I never told her, but she really looked funny in that suit, and so vulnerable with her stomach sticking straight out. Although her original intention was to stay as active as possible throughout the entire pregnancy, her large stomach was beginning to interfere with her job performance. This was the beginning of the end at work, and Dawn's supervisors were obviously concerned.

"Do you want to work in the office?" they asked.

"Absolutely not!" she responded.

"Then you need to get a doctors evaluation."

"I'll go today," she replied.

The doctor wrote down an extensive list of the activities that Dawn was able to perform, and the ones that she was definitely supposed to avoid.

After receiving the paperwork from Dawn's doctor, her supervisors called her into the office and said,"You're going on light duty."

That meant no rescues, and she could no longer be stationed at a lifeguard tower by herself. Looking back, I think this really crushed her. Dawn had a lot of pride, and was always considered one of the most physically active and respected

Dawn at Treasure Shores with co-workers

lifeguards on the beach.

Dawn requested to work at Wabasso Beach because it was busy. Her assignment was to watch the beach, while the other lifeguard performed the rescues. It went well until one crowded Saturday. She was working with her friend, Ron, a muscular guard in his mid twenties, when all hell broke loose. Although it was a beautiful day, with the temperature in the eighties and not a cloud in the sky, the ocean was treacherous. There were powerful two to three foot waves slamming on the shore, and strong rip currents developing up and down the beach.

Suddenly, while Dawn and Ron were sitting on the deck of the lifeguard tower, they noticed a swimmer in distress. He was seventy-five yards south of the tower caught in a rip current. Ron instantly jumped down onto the sand, ran to the water, and dove in. He swam as quickly as possible to the struggling victim as Dawn watched intently.

Then, to her dismay, someone else yelled, "Help!"

Dawn turned to the north and noticed another bather caught in a strong rip. The current was swift, and he was quickly being pulled out to sea. He tried to swim against the current, but was unable to make any headway. A large wave broke over top of him, pinning him underwater for a few seconds. When he surfaced he continued to struggle frantically, and it was obvious he was in dire need of help.

After catching his breath, he yelled again, "Over... here!"

He was trying desperately to stay afloat.

Without hesitation, Dawn blew her whistle, Beep, beep, beep, while putting up the red flag to alert the other bathers that she was leaving the tower. It is Indian River County's procedure to pull all bathers out of the water when there is no lifeguard watching the swimmers.

Dawn jumped down from the tower, rescue buoy in hand. She sprinted to the waters edge, walked gingerly sideways through the powerful shore break to avoid injuring her pregnant stomach, then dove into the warm murky water. When she surfaced, she began swimming with her head above water, trying not to lose sight of the victim. She managed to get within five feet of the flailing victim, stopped, and used the rotary kick to tread water.

"Calm down!" she told him in a stern voice.

He panicked and tried to grab her, but Dawn backed away quickly. Her fear was that he would take her under.

"Relax," she said.

Struggling, he went under for a second, swallowed water, surfaced, and started gasping for air. Dawn seized the opportunity and quickly jammed the rescue buoy into his chest.

"Hold on!" she shouted.

He clutched onto it tightly as she towed him out of the strong rip current.

When they were out of danger and safely on the beach, he took one look at Dawn and asked, "Are you pregnant?"

"About five months," she replied.

He was six feet tall, about thirty years old with a husky

frame, and was flabbergasted that he had been rescued by a pregnant lifeguard.

Then Dawn said, "I need some information for my report."

Embarrassed, he refused and quickly left the area.

Ron came sprinting up several seconds later, and said to Dawn, "Are you Ok?"

"Of course," she replied.

The news of Dawn's rescue spread quickly among the guards, and before the day was over, her supervisors were on their way to investigate the incident. Although Dawn did what she thought was right, from that day on it was determined that she would be stationed at either Golden Sands or Treasure Shores Beach. These beaches had the least amount of rescue activity and drew the smallest crowds. The only saving grace was that most of the time, Dawn was stationed with one of her best friends, Al. He was the oldest lifeguard on the force, standing only five feet three, but very strong and fit for his size. They were both hired by Indian River County on the same date, and had a similar workout ethic.

Dawn was bored out of her mind with her new light duty assignment. The only thing that she had to look forward to was her modified workout schedule. Everyday, she would take an ocean swim, short run or walk, followed by calisthenics. The morning was probably her favorite time of day. After she helped set up the lifeguard tower and checked the ocean conditions, she would swim a thousand yards before the tourists arrived. Her routine started approximately seventy-five to a hundred yards from the beach, just beyond the breakers. She would swim parallel to the beach using the crawl stroke. When she was finished, she would always call me, sounding so happy and invigorated after her workout.

I looked forward to her call every morning. She would tell me how the swim relieved the pressure on her stomach and how good it felt. Hearing her voice would always light up my day. Although I knew she was aware of the dangers and had more experience life guarding, I would always inquire about her safety, asking her about the bait fish and the sharks.

She usually responded in an annoyed voice with, "Don't be a nag!" or "Don't you trust my judgement?"

I did trust her, but being her husband, I couldn't help myself. Dawn was swimming pregnant with her belly hanging down beneath the surface, and it frightened me.

"There are sharks out there!" I would tell her.

"The sharks are always there," she would respond. "I watch mothers with their small babies playing in the surf everyday. Is there any difference?"

Dawn was right, but six months earlier I had a bad experience swimming at Wabasso Beach, and it haunted me.

One day while visiting Dawn at the Wabasso Beach lifeguard tower, I decided to go for my routine exercise swim. I love open water swims. It makes me feel free when my body is suspended on the surface, and sometimes when the conditions are right, I can even see the reef below.

This particular day the beach was packed and there were tourists everywhere.

"Dawn, would you like to go for a swim?" I asked.

"I can't," she replied.

Ordinarily, Dawn could join me on her break, but not this time. It was just too busy.

"I'm going out for a short swim," I told her.

She nodded her head.

I walked past the lifeguard board, a board designed to inform beach goers about current ocean conditions and any special hazards. Although I didn't notice any hazards listed, the yellow flag was flying from the lifeguard tower. The yellow flag warned bathers to use caution upon entering the water, and was routinely flown unless the conditions were perfect. I maneuvered my way past beach balls, umbrellas, and sunbathers sprawled out on the sand, then stood at the waters edge as the warm water rushed over my feet. I panned the area for anything unusual. There were no waves, and the ocean was a consistent aqua from the beach to the horizon.

My intention was to swim straight out about a quarter of a mile using the crawl stroke, and back again. It was my normal fifteen minute swim. I put on my goggles, walked into the water until I was waist deep, and dove in. Although the ocean looked clear, it turned out to be silty, and I was only able to see several feet in front of me. But that didn't stop me, and besides, there were no signs of sharks or bait fish anywhere. For the first few strokes, I didn't push it, but when I felt warmed up I gave it my all. With each stroke, I would pull as hard as I could, propelling myself through the water with ease. I swam for eight minutes, then stopped to see how far I had gone. I took off my goggles while treading water, and looked back toward the beach. The lifeguard tower looked small, and I could hear a faint laughter coming from the bathers playing in the surf.

What a feeling, being all alone in the vastness of the ocean. It felt so good that I decided to go farther. I swam at least another hundred yards in a deep trance thinking about Dawn. Then, without warning, my silence was broken.

Something large bumped me and I was spun partially around.

Startled..., I yelled out, "Dawn?"

I stopped and frantically looked about... hoping that it was Dawn playing with me.

"It can't be her," I thought.

"Shit!!!"

I knew what it was and began to panic.

"It's coming back!"

I prayed to myself that I was wrong. With my heart pounding and a knot in my throat, I turned toward the lifeguard tower and swam an Olympic pace back to shore. When I reached the beach, I sprinted to the lifeguard tower with a frightened expression on my face.

"Did you see what happened?" I asked Dawn, trying to catch my breath.

"I saw you enter the water just north of the guarded area, and watched you swim out," she said, "but I didn't notice anything unusual."

"I just got bumped!" I said excitedly.

"What do you mean?" she asked.

"Something large hit my leg and spun me around," I told her.

"You're kidding."

Bent over with my hands on my knees, still trying to catch my breath, I said, "Do I look like I'm kidding?"

Dawn knew I was upset and, with a concerned look on her face, she asked, "Are you Ok?"

"Yeah, I'll be all right," I responded.

Although as time passed I was able to joke about the incident, it was an experience that I definitely will never forget.

Chapter 13

It was October and Dawn and I desperately needed a vacation together. She was tired of not being able to physically go all out, and I needed a break from working and worrying about her pregnancy. We had both come from the north originally. Dawn was born in Connecticut and I lived in New Jersey for the first thirty years of my life, so when Dawn's physical activity level slowed down, we both yearned for the change of seasons. Maybe it was because of our favorite trip to Gatlinburg when we first met, I'm not sure, but after that trip, Dawn often commented on the beauty of the mountains and the smell and colors of the leaves. It was such a contrast to our normal life style.

On the first day of our vacation, we woke up early, packed our bags, maternity clothes and all, and left for the mountains. Although the chalet we rented on our first trip was no longer

The log cabin we stayed in

available, we were able to find a cozy rental nearby. It was a secluded, one bedroom log cabin near Hot Springs, North Carolina, located on a three-hundred-acre farm, overlooking the mountains. It had a stone fireplace, loft, an old rickety porch with two rocking chairs, and a great view.

We had a week to hike and play in the mountains. It felt so good just being alone together. Many people are afraid of retiring and being together constantly - not me. I could spend every minute of my whole life with Dawn.

The first morning, we woke up just before sunrise. The air was cool and crisp with the temperature in the lower forties, and there was a light dew covering the field of green grass in front of the cabin. After eating breakfast, we took a long hike on the farm, and happened upon a wooded path that led up a mountain. It was an old abandoned, dirt road carved into the mountainside, with steep drop offs and fallen trees blocking any motorized traffic. We maneuvered our way up the overgrown path for several hours. Although the sun was partially blocked by the heavy foliage, we could still see that the sky was mostly clear with small patches of white puffy clouds. Autumn was at its peak, with a brilliant array of colors ranging from yellow to red, and the wind was howling through the trees as the leaves fell softly all around us.

Dawn took a deep breath and said, "I love the smell of fall." It was her favorite time of year and she looked so content. At one point we stopped to shoot a hand gun, something Dawn had always wanted to try.

"Hold it with two hands," I told her.

She looked so funny with her big belly, trying to balance the gun in front of her. She squeezed the trigger and several rounds quickly went off, almost knocking her to the ground.

"You're dangerous," I said with a serious expression.

I tried to keep a straight face, but when we looked at each other, we just laughed. Dawn was determined, and wanted

Dawn shooting a handgun while pregnant

to try it again.

"Hold on tight," I instructed. "That's it. Put one leg in front of the other, now spread them a little farther."

When she looked ready, I backed up so she wouldn't fall on top of me.

Bang, Bang! Bang, Bang!

She shot a whole magazine of bullets, then finally stopped because of the loud noise echoing in the mountains.

We decided to rest for awhile before heading back, so we found a dry spot in the leaves and laid there next to each other, staring up at the sky.

"The warmth of the sun feels so good," Dawn said.

The peaceful sound of the birds chirping and the leaves rustling gently in the breeze almost put us to sleep.

"Let's head back," I suggested. "I'm getting hungry."

When we reached the cabin, we both sprawled on the couch next to each other.

After resting for a few moments, Dawn said, "Let's eat, then take a nap."

"Sounds good to me," I replied.

After lunch, we closed all the curtains, went up to the loft, and collapsed in bed. For some reason, I'll never forget that afternoon nap. Maybe it was the cool, fall breeze coming through the window, I'm not really sure, but Dawn looked so content lying sound asleep in my arms. The feel of her skin and the smell of her hair are still in my memory.

Toward the end of the week we wanted to try something exciting, so I suggested white-water rafting. We thought it was relatively safe compared to surfing. When we arrived at the rafting company, they took one look at Dawn's stomach and laughed. Disappointed, we left.

The next day, Dawn and I had a plan to conceal her pregnancy. Since the weather was cool, we tried to hide her protruding stomach with a winter coat. We went to a white-water canoeing company located on the French Broad River, in Hot Springs, North Carolina. We parked our pickup about fifty yards from the river in a small dirt parking lot, next to an old trailer that was resting on cinder blocks. Normally the parking lot was full, but not in the fall, as most of the rafting companies had already closed for the season. We walked up to the front stoop and saw a stack of canoes that had obviously not been used for quite awhile.

The trailer looked abandoned, but I knocked on the door anyway, and called out, "Is anyone there?"

Calvin answered the door. He was a slender man in his mid-thirties with an unkempt beard, dressed in cargo pants and sandals. Calvin, a native of the area, had rented me canoes in the past.

"What can I do for you?" he asked.

"Calvin, don't you recognize me?" I said. "I've rented canoes from you several times before."

He looked at me again, and said, "It's Bill from Florida."

While shaking hands, I introduced Dawn, "This is my wife.

We were married in the spring of last year."

"Nice meeting you," he said. "What brings you here this time of the year?"

"This is the last day of our vacation, and we'd like to rent a canoe."

"We haven't had much rain and the river is pretty low," he said.

"We don't care," I replied. "I just want to show Dawn the river."

He pulled a canoe off the pile, gave us each an oar and a life jacket, and asked, "Do you remember how to get to the pick up area across from Murray Branch Park?"

"Is that where you picked me up last time?" I asked.

"That's right. I'll be there in three hours. That'll give you plenty of time to enjoy the scenery," he said.

Calvin helped us carry the canoe to the riverbank.

"See you in awhile," he said as he walked away.

The air was cool and damp coming off the river, and we could hear the rapids roaring in the distance. I hesitated for a moment, wondering if we were doing the right thing.

"What are you waiting for?" Dawn asked.

I pushed the canoe part-way into the water.

"Get in," I told her.

She climbed over the back seat, grabbed her oar, and sat down.

"Hurry up, let's go!" she said playfully.

I pushed the canoe out until it was deep enough to float both of us, then jumped into the back seat. We maneuvered our way through the shallow rocks to the swift current, then took off and headed swiftly down the lower section of the French Broad River. Dawn was grinning from ear to ear. The lower section starts at the bridge in Hot Springs and winds westward toward Tennessee. It's not quite as challenging as the upper section of the river, but it can still be a lot of fun.

After only three hundred yards, we were headed for the biggest rapid on the lower section when, just before the point of no return, we hit a large boulder that was hidden under the surface of the water. It turned our canoe sideways.

"Paddle hard to the right!" I shouted, while trying to stabilize and steer the canoe at the same time.

We tried to line ourselves up straight but didn't have time.

"Damn it!" I shouted. "Hold on!"

We held tightly onto the sides of the canoe, bracing ourselves.

I heard Dawn scream, "...We're gonna tip!"

"Whoah, whoah!" we shouted, as we bounced over one critical section of rocks to the next.

Once we got caught in the swift current, it quickly pulled us through the entire rapid, spitting us out at the bottom.

"Great ride!" Dawn shouted.

"We're lucky we didn't flip," I replied anxiously.

After becoming familiar with the canoe, we managed to paddle through the remaining rapids with ease and made it to the pick up area in just over two hours.

"Let's hang out here," I suggested. "Calvin won't be coming for quite awhile."

We paddled to a huge willow tree that was alongside the riverbank, and held onto its long slender limbs.

"Let's do it again," Dawn said. "That was fun."

It wasn't like the ocean, but the river provided her with that thrill ride she had been craving. Dawn couldn't live without being active or experiencing some type of excitement. When we returned to the cabin that evening, Dawn and I sat on the porch staring at the mountains as they changed colors with the sunset, talking about our future.

The week ended with a ten hour drive home, but to Dawn and me the trip didn't seem long at all. We reminisced for hours about our vacation. She mentioned the canoe ride down the rapids over and over again. To this day, I don't believe that Calvin knew Dawn was pregnant.

I thought a lot about that afternoon nap in the cabin, realizing how compatible we were. Our future looked promising. Both of us felt that our future children had no choice but to grow up happy, and we made it our goal to give them the opportunity to experience life as we did - to the fullest.

Chapter 14

When we crossed the Eau Gallie Causeway onto the barrier island, we could see the ocean in the distance. The sun was setting and the sky had an orange tint to it with clouds ranging from purple to dark blue. After only one weeks vacation, we had missed the vastness and the beauty of the sea. Central Florida was our home and we loved it. As we drove along A1A, we could see the waves peeling off in perfect formation along the coast.

"Did you see that left?" I asked Dawn.

There was a huge ground swell, with waves lining up over a quarter mile long. A ground swell is a powerful wave created by large weather disturbances off shore.

"It's at least head high," she replied. "Why don't you go out when we get home."

Although I wanted to surf badly, I knew it would be too dark by the time we arrived. Besides, I was exhausted from the long drive.

We pulled in our driveway, unpacked, ate, and went directly to bed. The next morning I woke up just after sunrise and called Nick. My younger brother by seven years, he stood six-feet-two with curly dark brown hair and dark brown eyes. Nick had big muscular legs and hated wearing shoes.

"Are you up for a morning surf session?" I asked.

"How are the waves?" he asked.

"Last night on our way home they were about two-to-three feet and glassy, and I'm sure they're still good," I said.

"I'll ride down and take a look," Nick said.

Nick lived two blocks north of my house, and within ten minutes he called back and said, "Let's go!"

"Meet me at my house in five minutes," I said enthusiastically.

I got off the phone and immediately called my friend Dave, a neighbor that I often surfed with. He was six feet, built like a baseball player, and had a southern drawl with a laid back personality.

"Hi, Dave. What are you doing this morning?" I asked.

"Nothing really," he replied.

Dave was a fisherman at heart, but loved surfing large glassy waves.

"The waves are great. Nick and I are going out."

"Where are you going?" he asked.

He didn't like surfing with large crowds, preferring our hometown break.

"Right out front. Want to go?"

He agreed instantly, and said, "I'll pick you up in a few minutes."

Nick came over and we donned our wetsuits before Dave arrived.

Within minutes Dave pulled up in front of the driveway, blew his horn, and said, "let's go!"

We threw our boards into the back of his pickup, jumped in, and took off.

In less than three minutes, we pulled into the Floridana Beach parking lot. We grabbed our boards, rushed down to the beach, and were surprised to see there was no one else out. The waves looked great, but we could see dark clouds of bait fish everywhere.

"What do you think?" Nick asked me apprehensively.

Looking at the waves peel off, I said, "Let's go for it."

We quickly waxed our boards and took the plunge. As soon as our surfboards hit the cold murky water, bait fish scattered beneath us. Until that moment, I don't think we realized how bad it really was. Mullet were everywhere! We paddled as quickly as we could to get beyond the shore break and out of the trough where the large schools of bait fish were grouping.

"I'm gonna make it out easily," I thought.

Then, just as I entered the impact zone (the area where the waves break), I looked up and saw a large wave barreling down on top of me... I took a deep breath, and attempted to duck dive under the crashing wave.

Booom!!!

It hit me so hard that it knocked me off my board, and pinned me to the bottom.

"Ah...shit!"

I could feel mullet brushing against my body.

"I've gotta get out of here," I said to myself.

Finally, my leash, which was attached to my ankle and surfboard, jerked my leg as the wave passed by and I was able to surface. I quickly scrambled back onto my board and paddled as hard as I could to safety, just beyond the impact zone.

Sitting on my surfboard next to Dave waiting for a wave, we saw shark fins and the silver bellies of tarpon all around us.

"Watch Out, Dave!" I shouted.

A shark swam right by his board, and he quickly lifted his legs to avoid being bitten.

"Damn!" he said, with a frightened look on his face.

This was turning out to be one of the scariest days that I had ever surfed. As I sat there on my surfboard surrounded by bait fish, I began thinking and worrying about Dawn.

"Dawn can't go swimming," I thought.

Tomorrow was her first day back at work, and I knew she was dying to go for her routine exercise swim. I imagined Dawn swimming laps surrounded by bait fish, tarpon, and sharks with our little child in her stomach. Just the thought of it made me feel anxious. My thoughts were suddenly interrupted by Nick.

"I'm done. It's not worth it!" he said while paddling to shore.

Dave and I knew what Nick meant and followed closely

behind. On the way in I thought about how lucky we were. None of us had gotten struck by a tarpon or, worse yet, attacked by a shark. Reaching the shore, we all gave a sigh of relief.

"That's the worst I've ever seen it," Nick said as we walked over the boardwalk.

I nodded my head and said, "It was pretty crazy."

When we reached the parking lot, we loaded our boards onto Dave's truck and headed home. I couldn't stop worrying about Dawn swimming the next day.

When we reached the house, I said good-bye, grabbed my board, and rushed inside to find Dawn.

"Dawn!" I yelled.

She didn't answer. I walked into the kitchen and found her sitting at the table.

"DAWN, YOU CAN'T GO SWIMMING TOMORROW!"

She jumped out of her chair with a pissed off look on her face.

"You're starting already," she said defensively. "We just got home."

"There were sharks and bait fish everywhere!"

She didn't want to hear it, and sat back down with an indifferent look on her face. I tried again to tell her.

"There were fins thrashing through the water, and Dave almost got bitten on the leg."

She still didn't respond. I thought to myself that there was no way I could let her swim tomorrow - I had to stop her.

She looked at me, shook her head, and turned away. It seemed like she didn't care about the bait fish, tarpon, or even the sharks, but I knew that wasn't true. Although I had badgered her about swimming during her entire pregnancy, I had to make her understand that this time was different.

Later that evening when we had both calmed down, Dawn said, "Sharks are always in the water. You're just going to have to trust my judgement."

"I do trust you, but you don't understand how bad it was," I pleaded.

"We've had this conversation a hundred times before," she replied angrily. "I'll check the conditions and if there are any signs of sharks or bait fish, I won't go in. Ok?"

I stopped the conversation because I knew I was getting nowhere, and went to bed frustrated.

Chapter 15

It was six a.m. on October 26th and my alarm went off. I sprung out of bed, shut off the alarm, turned on the shower, and jumped in. As I stood there with the water hitting my back, I had a sick feeling inside. I was still concerned about Dawn swimming and I couldn't get it off my mind.

"She doesn't realize how bad it is." I thought.

Before I went out the door, I tried one more time to convince her.

I woke her up, saying "Rocky (a nickname I often called her)... Rocky - please don't go swimming today."

She seemed annoyed and didn't respond. I said it again to make sure that she heard and understood what I was saying.

"Please...don't go out!!!"

She heard me all right. She just looked at me, rolled her eyes and sighed. I left the house knowing she was going swimming. She was so damn stubborn.

Later that morning, Dawn gathered her belongings and went to work. She was assigned to Treasures Shores Beach. This was the northern most guarded beach in Indian River County. She had Jake as a partner that day, a young lifeguard in his early twenties who loved to surf. He stood about five-feet-ten, had a medium size frame with his bleached blonde hair cropped off just below the ears.

When Dawn arrived at the beach, she helped Jake prep the tower with all the necessary equipment, and set up the lifeguard information board. This was a three by four foot chalk board, used for listing ocean conditions and any special hazards, positioned at the end of the boardwalk. Dawn picked up the chalk and wrote down; wind, 0-5 mph; waves, 2-3 ft; visibility, 0-5 ft, and under special hazards; drop off, bait fish, tarpon, and sharks. When she finished, she climbed up into the tower, grabbed the yellow flag that was stored under the wooden bench inside, and stuck it in the flag holder on the front deck. There were three different warning flags, red, yellow and green. A red warning flag was flown when there was no swimming allowed, while yellow indicated swimming was permitted, but warned bathers to use caution because some hazards may exist, and green meant that the conditions were favorable for swimming with clear water, no currents, bait fish, or any other special hazards. Everyday before 9:00 am, it was the responsibility of the on duty lifeguards to fill out the Lifeguard Safety Board and to raise the appropriate flag.

After the tower was set up, Dawn wanted to take her normal morning swim. She stood on the deck of the lifeguard tower for ten minutes, checking in both directions for any sign of sharks.

"It looks Ok. He's such a worry wart," she thought. "Besides, I would let other mothers and their children swim in the water."

Dawn felt it was completely safe to go swimming.

She turned toward Jake, who was sitting inside the tower reading and listening to a new cassette he had just purchased, and said, "I'm going for a swim."

He nonchalantly looked up at Dawn.

"Let me know if you see any bait fish," Dawn said.

"Ok," he answered.

Jake knew her routine, everyone did. Dawn got down from the tower using the rescue ramp, which extended from the lifeguard tower straight down to the beach.

Dawn walked to the waters edge still thinking about my warning.

Panning the water one more time, she said, "There aren't

any bait fish."

The only sign of life on the beach was an older couple sitting on a blanket in the sand. It was a typical quiet fall day. Dawn put on her yellow swim cap, goggles, and put her rescue buoy over her shoulder. She was ready - I can picture her face - she loved it. To avoid any damage to her pregnant belly, Dawn slowly walked into the water timing her entry into the shore break... Did the bait fish scatter as she lowered herself into the water? I'll never know. The water was murky and it was difficult for Dawn to see. She took a couple of strokes and her pregnant body was finally weightless on the surface of the water. Dawn thought how good it felt.

"Finally, relief - no more pressure on my back," she thought.

Dawn swam several more strokes, reached the impact zone and stopped. She began treading water in an effort to time the large waves passing through. She selected a good wave to dive under and came up safely on the other side. Dawn's goggles were fogged from the cool water, so she stopped to clear them.

Her intention was to swim at least 1000 yards, turning around every 200 yards. This was her normal routine. She started her swim by heading south toward Golden Sands Beach using the crawl stroke.

Were there bait fish?

Or worse yet...?

She had no way of knowing... swimming through the murky unknown.

To this day, I can imagine her slicing through the water with her big stomach hanging down beneath the surface. Just the thought of it makes me nauseous.

Several minutes passed... Dawn was now about half way through her first 200 yard lap. She was in a trance... As she swam, Dawn thought about our trip to Gatlinburg, the baby, our future together.

Bam!!!

She never finished her thought. All of a sudden, Dawn was slammed so hard that her ears were ringing from the collision - it felt like she had been hit by a large truck!

"What the hell!"

"What's going on?"

Dawn lifted her head out of the water and scanned the beach to get her bearings.

"Where am I?" she asked herself.

She had been completely spun in the opposite direction. It confused her. She treaded water in a daze and attempted to gain her composure. After a couple of seconds..., Dawn realized what had happened. She knew!

SHARK!!!

Her left leg and hand started to burn, and her pregnant stomach felt like it had taken a severe blow. Her mind began racing.

"The baby!!!"

"God, let the baby be OK!"

Dawn lifted her left hand out of the water.

"It's bad," she said to herself.

Blood was dripping from her severely lacerated wrist and fingers. They were torn up so badly that she wouldn't be able to swim with them. Her attention was drawn to her stomach - her body was trembling uncontrollably. She looked into the water in an attempt to see more of her injuries, but it was too murky. Dawn ran her hand over her stomach, but couldn't feel any damage.

"The water around me is turning bloody red."

"I hate to look... but I have to."

Dawn rolled onto her right side, and instantly saw the huge gaping, jagged gash on her left leg - it was the perfect shape of a shark's mouth.

"Oh my God!"

Now her attention was drawn to her unborn child. Dawn

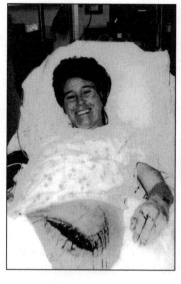

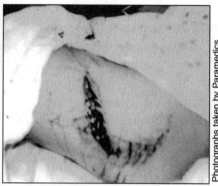

Dawn's shark attack wound

*Dawn in the hospital
after her shark attack*

floated on her back to examine her stomach and didn't see any visible damage.

Everything seemed like it was moving in slow motion. She knew that she had better get out of the water as soon as possible. She was concerned that the shark would come back. She panned the water around her searching for a shark fin to surface. No sign anywhere - yet. Immediately, Dawn turned toward the lifeguard tower and gave the rescue signal to Jake.

She blew her whistle three times, while she held her arms in a circle over her head. This meant call 911 immediately and assist in a rescue.

"Come on, Jake!" she said to herself.

He did not respond. She tried again to signal him.

Beep Beep Beep!!

Beeeeeeeeeeeeep!!!

She screamed as loud as she could, "Jake!"

Still no response. Dawn looked up and down the beach hoping someone had seen or heard her call for help. Realizing that she was on her own, she began to panic. She started to cry...

and began to hyperventilate. For the first time in her life, Dawn was really frightened.

"The shark is coming back..." she thought.

Dawn pictured in her mind a large menacing shark charging from the deep without any warning....Overwhelmed, she thought she was going to die.

"Mom... Mom!!!" her thoughts called out, while she sobbed in desperation.

Then she said to herself, "Calm down and breathe." Dawn realized she had no choice but to rescue herself. She became angry at the situation and began to gather her strength.

Awkwardly, Dawn started swimming to shore without the full use of either her left leg or left hand. She used the side stroke keeping her head out of the water. The beach never looked so far away and she was terrified. It felt like an eternity.

As she swam, she kept looking for a shark fin to surface, and prayed as she left a large trail of blood behind her, which, she feared, the shark might follow. She finally reached the point where the waves were breaking. Normally, because of her pregnancy, she would carefully choose which wave to ride to shore, but not this time. Dawn dove into the first wave - she was desperate. It pushed her only part way in. Her big belly was dragging in the water and slowed her progress down. The next wave pinned her under water, and she scrambled frantically to get to the surface. The thought of being under water with that menacing shark terrified her. The third wave pushed her into the deep drop-off a few feet from the beach. She could stand, but the water was up to her chest.

Because of the awkwardness of her stomach and her injuries, Dawn struggled trying to get onto the beach. She tried several times, but couldn't make it. She would have to wait for a wave to help push her up. Dawn was frantic waiting in the water for the next wave. Being submerged was really getting to her. She wanted out... away from that shark! Finally, she could see a set of waves slowly approaching. Dawn's plan was to jump up into a wave so it would push her onto the beach - timing was everything. As the wave approached, she worried about the shark being in it.

"I have no choice. I need to get out of the water!"

Dawn positioned herself with her knees partially bent and, just before the wave broke, jumped into it. The wave threw her onto the beach. Still partially in the water, she began to crawl to safety.

Bam!

A large wave hit her on the back and startled her. Dawn thought it was the shark again, but then realized what had happened. Shook, she continued to crawl out of the water. Another wave hit her feet and she jumped, but this time she was able to crawl the rest of the way out.

"I finally made it!" she said with a huge sigh of relief.

Once on the beach, Dawn again tried to get Jake's attention by using the rescue signal.

Beep Beep Beep!

Still no response.

"He can't hear it! I have to get closer." she thought.

She pulled off her rescue buoy, goggles, and cap, and began hobbling toward the lifeguard tower, blowing the whistle the entire way. When she was about a hundred yards from the tower, Jake finally responded. He came running out onto the deck of the tower with a horrified look on his face. An older gentleman on the beach also came running toward her to help.

"Call 911!" Dawn yelled to Jake.

"I'VE BEEN ATTACKED BY A SHARK!"

Jake was stunned and hurried back inside the tower to call 911. Dawn pulled her way up the ramp using the railings, and began limping back and forth on the deck. She was still in survival mode, with her heart racing.

Jake got off the phone and said, "Sit down!"

"Call Bill!" she said.

Dawn sat in amazement as she leaned back against the tower. "I can't believe it!"

"A few minutes ago I was almost killed by a shark."

She knew that her stomach wasn't cut, but the severe blow from the shark attack had her concerned about her unborn child. After calling me, Jake began to bandage her arm - blood was everywhere. The phone rang in the tower and he had to stop.

"Treasure Shores," Jake said.

"This is dispatch," a lady said in an official tone. "We need more information about the victim for the paramedics."

The bleeding was not stopping, and Dawn quickly grabbed the phone from Jake so he could finish bandaging her wounds.

"Hello" Dawn said.

"...This is dispatch. We need more information for the paramedics," she repeated. "Where are the victims wounds?"

In a reasonably calm voice while looking down at her leg, Dawn said, "The left leg and left arm."

"How deep are they?"

Dawn lowered the receiver, and asked Jake, "How deep is the wound on my leg?"

"Three inches," Jake said as he continued to bandage her arm.

"Three inches," Dawn repeated to dispatch.

"What about the wound to her arm?"

"There's a laceration on the wrist that's about an inch deep, and numerous lacerations across the fingers."

"How coherent is the patient?"

Dawn said, "You're talking to her."

There was silence...

"What do you mean?"

"You're talking to the shark attack victim. My partner is bandaging me up."

The dispatcher sounded amazed and said, "I'll radio the paramedics about your condition... They're already en route."

My station, Indian River Shores Public Safety Department, was approximately ten miles down the road. I was the Lieutenant in charge of the shift that day. Jake had called me on the phone at approximately 10 a.m., right in the middle of a training session. I remember Jake saying in a very calm voice, "Dawn has been attacked by a shark."

"Are you kidding?" I asked.

"No."

I said, "Jake, you're full of shit! That's not funny," and hung up.

The reason I didn't believe Jake was his unusual calmness and the tone of his voice. When I went back into the bay of the fire station to finish our training session, our station tones went off. The tones go off to signal us when there is an emergency call in our zone.

I'll never forget that particular alarm as long as I live.

I heard the tone signaling our station, followed by a voice saying "Indian River Shores Rescue 104 respond to Treasure Shores Beach. A pregnant lifeguard has been attacked by a shark and is going to be airlifted off the beach."

I was shocked and my friends just looked at me in disbelief. Bill, a sergeant from my department said, "Bill, let me take you!" I guess he knew that if I drove I would either kill myself or, worse yet, some innocent bystander. We jumped into his patrol car and raced toward Treasure Shores. I don't think Bill and I said a word to each other the entire trip; my mind was racing, wondering what the hell happened.

I prayed to myself, "God, please let Dawn and the baby be OK!"

Then I got mad.

"Dawn, you're so damn stubborn! Why didn't you listen?" I thought.

I tried to block out the possible consequences. The whole situation didn't seem real. My hands started trembling as I fought back tears.

"I have to help Dawn and our baby! She needs my strength." Just before we reached the intersection of A1A and 510 at Wabasso Beach, we saw an ambulance cross in front of us. It was from Indian River County Station 5, located on the west side of the intra-coastal waterway. We were right behind it as we approached the entrance to Treasure Shores Beach access when, to our surprise, the County ambulance passed the entrance.

I quickly got on the radio, my voice quivering in fear, and said, "You just missed the entrance!"

We made a right turn into the park with our wheels squealing, and when we reached the boardwalk that led to the lifeguard tower, Bill slammed on his brakes. Being the first rescue person on scene and Dawn's husband, I felt totally out of control. I knew that Dawn had to be in serious trouble, and tried to compose myself as I jumped out of the front side passenger door and ran up the walkway.

On the way up, an older couple passed me and the man yelled, "You better hurry - It's bad!"

I finally made it to the tower and saw Dawn for the first time. Jake was trying to place a large bandage on her leg to stop the bleeding. Dawn looked down at me as I climbed up the ladder, and gave a big sigh of relief.

"She looks out of it!" I thought.

Dawn knew that I would take care of her, but she had no clue how anxious I was.

I asked her, "How are you doing?"

What a dumb question.

She attempted a smile and said, "Ok, I guess."

There was blood all over the lifeguard tower. Dawn literally looked in shock. Her color was bad. I gave her a big hug wishing I could take her place. She felt clammy and her body was shaking uncontrollably. As I helped Jake bandage Dawn's leg and arm, rescue personnel arrived in full force. The paramedics from Station 5 took over. They started an IV line and finished bandaging her wounds. It was very difficult for me not to show emotion... Dawn was my lifelong companion, and I was really afraid for her.

Everyone worked as quickly as possible, knowing that Dawn was six and a half months pregnant and there could be serious complications with the baby.

"What's the ETA (estimated time of arrival) of the helicopter?" one of the medics radioed dispatch.

"About twenty minutes," the dispatcher responded.

"Cancel the helicopter. We can't wait that long," the medic said. "We'll take her to Indian River Memorial Hospital by ambulance."

"10-4," dispatch responded.

We strapped Dawn onto a backboard, a narrow wooden board with handles, carried her slowly down the rescue ramp, and made our way through the deep sand to the boardwalk. We put her onto a stretcher and rolled her to the parking lot. She appeared fairly stable, but once she was secured in the back of the ambulance, her condition began to deteriorate. The physical trauma and mental anxiety were beginning to take their toll.

"I feel nauseous," Dawn said shivering.

"Cover her up," a medic yelled.

I grabbed her hand and said, "Hang in there, Dawn."

Her skin felt cool and clammy, indicating that she was still in shock, and she appeared to be drifting off.

"Can you hear me, Dawn?" one of the medics asked.

She nodded her head, but she looked out of it.

"Keep talking to her," one of the medics said to me.

"Stay with me, Dawn," I said.

Time seemed to slow down for Dawn. As she watched everyone hustling around, she thought about the seriousness of the situation.

"I'm worried. I haven't felt the baby kick since the attack. That shark slammed into my stomach so hard... I lost a lot of blood. That can't be good. I feel like I'm fading. I can't let myself go to sleep. I need to stay awake for the sake of the baby... My hand and leg are starting to really hurt... I just wish they would get me to the hospital. God, I hope the baby is Ok."

One of the medics grabbed the transmitter to the radio, and called the emergency room to alert the staff of her condition.

"Med Five to Indian River Memorial Hospital."

"Go ahead Med Five."

"We'll be coming in with a pregnant patient who has been attacked by a large shark. She has a ten inch jagged laceration on her left thigh, and numerous deep lacerations to her left wrist and fingers with substantial blood loss. We have bandaged the wounds, started a large bore IV with normal saline, administered high flow oxygen, and have the patient packaged on a backboard."

"What's your ETA?" The emergency room dispatcher asked.

"We should be there in less than fifteen minutes."

With the lights and siren on and a police escort, we headed to the hospital. As we crossed over the Wabasso Causeway and onto US 1, Dawn was still in great distress, but after ten minutes of high-flow IV fluids and oxygen, miraculously her condition began to improve. By the time we reached the hospital, she began to stabilize.

"You're going to be Ok, Dawn," I said.

She didn't say a word. She looked up at me and tried to smile, but I could tell that she was still very concerned about the baby.

Chapter 16

T he paramedics opened the back doors of the ambulance and unloaded the stretcher. The entrance doors to the emergency room opened, and Dawn was rushed inside and rolled into a cubicle, which was fully equipped with a hospital bed, oxygen, IV pole and trays full of operating tools. The emergency room doctor and several nurses were awaiting her arrival.

"Ready, lift," a male nurse ordered as the medics and I lifted Dawn onto the examination bed.

A nurse pulled back the sheet covering Dawn, cut her bathing suit off, and helped her put a hospital gown on. The emergency room doctor and the nurses quickly started their examination. They began by conducting a thorough preliminary survey, checking her vital signs to see if she was still in shock.

"Her blood pressure is 110 over 60. Pulse 110 and regular," a nurse said. Considering the trauma and severe blood loss Dawn had just experienced, she appeared to be fairly stable.

"Continue high flow oxygen, and hook up a new bag of saline," the doctor ordered. "And get me the scissors."

He looked into Dawn's eyes with a flashlight, and asked, "What day is it?"

"Tuesday," Dawn answered.

"Did you ever lose consciousness?" he asked.

"No," she said.

He began palpating her body from her head down to her toes for any abnormalities.

A nurse handed the doctor the scissors, and he cut the large blood soaked bandage off her leg. For the first time the gaping, jagged gash on Dawn's left leg was exposed. The doctor probed and prodded the wound to determine the extent of the damage. He removed the bandages from her left hand. It was severely lacerated and mangled, and her fingers were swollen and twisted from the powerful jaws of the shark.

"Get her rings off," the doctor said to a nurse.

The nurse tried to slide Dawn's wedding ring off her finger with a lubricant, but was unsuccessful and had to cut it off with a string saw.

The doctor took off his gloves and said, "Because of the size and depth of your wounds, I am recommending that we get you a plastic surgeon."

"Whatever you think is best," Dawn said.

The doctor turned to the nurse and said, "Please call the plastic surgeon right away."

A crowd of doctors, nurses, and paramedics were beginning to gather around Dawn's bed. The wounds from her shark attack were not the typical injuries found in Florida, and it was obvious she had been attacked by a very large shark. I happened to overhear one of the hospital medics, a friend of mine and respected fisherman, talking about her attack.

"I've never seen a bite so large! She must have been bitten by a large 8 to 10 foot bull shark," he said.

Dawn's obstetrician arrived.

"Dawn, are you doing Ok?" she asked.

"I guess so," Dawn replied apprehensively.

The OB stood next to Dawn and began her examination by palpating Dawn's stomach and pelvic area. She pushed hard, and Dawn winced.

"Did that hurt?" the doctor asked.

"No, but it felt uncomfortable," Dawn said.

Next she listened for the baby's heartbeat with a stethoscope. Dawn looked so worried and helpless lying there that I fought back tears.

"Please let the baby be OK," I prayed.

The OB looked up at us and said, "I can hear a heartbeat!"

We were overwhelmed with joy. A nurse then attached a baby monitor to Dawn's stomach. It's a device that is placed on the abdomen, held in position with a strap, that shows contractions on a monitor. We watched nervously.

After her examination was finished, the OB took off her stethoscope and said, "The baby should be fine, but there are signs of uterine irritability. We'll have to continue to monitor you closely."

The OB's intentions were to examine Dawn more thoroughly after her surgery was complete.

Dawn's mother appeared at the door. She stood four feet eleven, had red hair, and a fair complexion. Dawn hugged her mom tightly. Dawn's body was trembling and her eyes were filled with emotion. She looked so little in her mother's arms.

"The baby should be OK!" Dawn told her mom.

The plastic surgeon arrived, and we watched intently as he consulted with the emergency room doctor and the OB. Then he turned to Dawn, introduced himself, pulled up a stool, and examined her wounds closely.

"I need to operate right away," he said.

"Will the baby be safe?" Dawn asked.

"There are always some risks during surgery, but the baby should be fine," he replied.

Fearing the anesthesia might harm the baby, Dawn said, "I don't want to be put under. Isn't there something else you can do?"

"I can use a local," the surgeon said. "But it will be very uncomfortable."

"I can handle it," Dawn said.

She would endure anything to help protect her unborn child. The nurse handed the surgeon a large needle of Novocaine. He began by injecting numerous shots into the large gash on her leg and into the deep lacerations on her wrist and fingers. Dawn was tough and didn't shed a tear. She only flinched as the needle was stuck directly into her wounds.

"It should take effect shortly," the surgeon said.

The surgeon left momentarily, and Dawn's lifeguard supervisors walked in. Apparently the emergency waiting room was filling up with news reporters from all over. The fact that Dawn was a full-time lifeguard and six and a half months pregnant, drew an incredibly large crowd. Her supervisors wanted to down play the incident and were very concerned what Dawn would say to the media. She consulted with her supervisors for several minutes. Dawn was very calm about the whole situation and handled herself like a professional.

A nurse interrupted, "I'm sorry, but it's time to leave."

Everyone quickly left, except for Dawn's mom and me. The surgeon returned wearing an operating gown. He scrubbed his hands in the sink, put on his gloves and a mask, and sat down next to Dawn.

"Tell me if you feel anything." he told Dawn.

He pulled the adjustable overhead light close to her. The doctor prodded Dawn's leg, checking for the effectiveness of the Novocaine. Dawn didn't say a word. A nurse, dressed in hospital greens and wearing a mask, handed the doctor a scalpel off the tray that was now positioned next to him. The room was completely quiet, and Dawn's eyes stared straight ahead. The surgeon cut away the jagged skin that was torn by the shark's razor sharp teeth. The wound was so deep that it took three layers of stitches to sew her leg back together. Next, he worked on her wrist and fingers. The shark had lacerated all of Dawn's fingers and torn open her wrist. The doctor was very concerned because of the numerous nerves located in the hand and the extensive damage from the shark bite. After the doctor stitched up her wrist, Dawn could no longer stand the pain of the surgery, so the doctor placed butterfly bandages over the rest of the wounds on her hand. The baby kicked during the whole procedure, adding to Dawn's anxiety.

The surgery seemed to last forever. When it was finished, Dawn had received over eighty-five stitches in her leg and numerous stitches and butterfly bandages on her fingers and wrist.

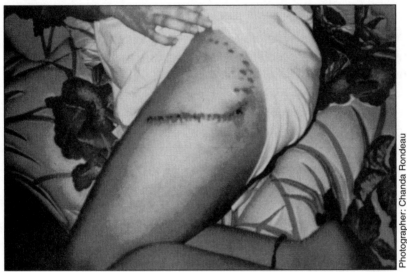

Photographer: Chanda Rondeau

Dawn's shark attack wound one day after surgery

"How are you feeling?" I asked Dawn.

"I'll be all right," she said.

The surgeon got up from his stool, took off his gloves, and pulled his mask below his chin.

"It went well, but there is a possibility of nerve damage. I couldn't detect any during the operation, the swelling made it difficult. We'll arrange for a follow-up exam after the swelling goes down."

"Thank you very much," I said, shaking his hand.

The hospital was under pressure to give a press release, so after Dawn's wounds were cleaned up and bandaged, she agreed to speak to the media. When the emergency room doors opened, Dawn's hospital bed was surrounded by reporters - television cameras were everywhere. They stuck a microphone in Dawn's face.

"What happened?" they asked.

"...The beaches are safe, my attack was caused by mistaken identity..." she told them.

She continued with a very factual account of the incident. When the cameras turned to me, I was so emotional that I don't remember what I said. Even the surgeon was asked numerous questions with a camera in his face.

After several minutes of being interviewed, Dawn was rushed out of the emergency room and taken to a birthing room in delivery, where she was again examined by her OB and placed on a baby monitor.

"The baby's heart beat is strong," the OB said. "But your uterus is still irritable."

The doctor gave Dawn an injection of Brethine, a smooth muscle relaxer, to calm her uterus.

"That should help," she said.

We sat for hours, hoping our unborn child would be Ok. The thought of our child being born prematurely frightened me. My oldest daughter, Kelli, who was born eight weeks prematurely, developed numerous complications after delivery. I was afraid that Dawn's situation, complicated by the trauma of the shark attack, might be much worse.

Late that evening, the OB returned to the room with Dawn's medical chart in hand.

"I'd like to send you home."

"Are you sure?" Dawn asked.

"You need a good night's sleep. It's important," the OB replied.

Although Dawn looked relieved, intuition told me that she should not go home.

Within minutes a nurse appeared in the doorway, and asked, "Are you feeling up to one more interview? It's a reporter from the local paper."

"Sure. Send him in," Dawn replied.

The reporter interviewed Dawn for quite awhile, and even took some pictures. As soon as he was finished, the nurse reappeared with a bag of prescriptions in her hand.

"The doctor has prescribed antibiotics to prevent any infection that might develop, and a medication to ease the pain," the nurse said.

Dawn was released shortly thereafter, and brought to the front entrance by wheel chair.

"Wait here. I'll get the pickup," I told Dawn.

I returned quickly, helped Dawn into the front seat, and took off.

"How are you feeling?" I asked over and over again.

When we were about halfway home she said, "It's really starting to throb."

It was obvious that as soon as the Novocaine began to wear off, Dawn started to feel the full effect of the shark attack and the surgery. By the time we got home, she looked emotionally drained. I helped her out of the pickup and into the house.

"Go to bed," I told her. "You need to rest."

When Dawn laid down it was a major feat to get comfortable. She had to lie awkwardly because of her leg wound and pregnant belly, and repositioned herself over and over again.

Finally, after I thought she was situated, I asked, "Can I get you anything?"

"I need something to elevate my left arm," she answered.

Every time she lowered her arm, the blood rushing to it would shoot excruciating pain into her hand. I found some extra pillows and stacked them alongside her to elevate her arm.

"Does that feel better?" I asked.

"Yes, that should be fine," she said.

She looked so agitated lying there that I thought she would never fall asleep, but after the pain medication kicked in, she dozed off.

"What a day this has been," I said to myself.

The next morning Dawn woke up early.

"How are you feeling?" I asked.

"Fine, except for the pains in my lower back. Would you mind massaging it."

"Describe the pain," I said, while rubbing her back.

"I have a dull ache in my lower back, almost like a menstrual cramp," she answered.

A few moments later she said, "You can stop rubbing now, the pain went away."

Realizing what it was, I said,"You're having contractions! We need to get to the doctor's office right away."

My worst nightmare had come true. She was going into premature labor. Dawn and I quickly got dressed and headed directly to the doctors office. As soon as we arrived, Dawn was put on a baby monitor, and the doctor confirmed our suspicion. "You're in labor," the OB told Dawn.

The doctor gave her a shot of Brethine and, after several hours, Dawn's contractions subsided.

The OB returned and said, "I'm sending you home, but this time you're on complete bed rest."

She handed Dawn a prescription for Brethine and told her to take one pill every six hours around the clock.

"You may feel a little jittery, but that's normal. If you have any problems, call me," she said.

I took Dawn home and she went right to bed. After only a couple of days, she began to feel the effects of the medication and her resting heart rate elevated to one hundred beats per minute. She had trouble focusing when trying to read, her hands trembled uncontrollably, and it was very difficult for her to get a good night's sleep. I felt so badly for her, but there was nothing I could do.

The medication worked well for about two weeks, and then one morning, her contractions broke through the medication. I drove Dawn to the doctor's office, and she was immediately taken into an examination room.

"You appear to be extremely dehydrated," the doctor said.

"I don't understand," Dawn said. "I drink plenty of water."

"It's probably from the trauma of the shark attack. Remember, you did lose a lot of blood... We'll give you some IV fluids. That should help," she said.

After four hours of fluids her contractions eased up, and she was sent home again, but this time her dosage of Brethine had to be increased to every four hours.

Two days before Thanksgiving, Dawn's contractions broke through the medication again, and this time she was admitted to the hospital. The doctor and nurses were waiting for us when we arrived at the delivery room. Dawn was once again examined and placed on a baby monitor. They administered a strong shot of Brethine, but it didn't work.

"Your contractions are increasing to a dangerous level. I'll have to put you on a magnesium oxide drip," the OB said.

This was a powerful drug administered through an intravenous line, that seemed to alter her level of consciousness.

"Everything looks blurry," Dawn mentioned over and over again.

Dawn was monitored very closely over the next couple of days and then, on Thanksgiving Day, her condition began to worsen. Her blood pressure was extremely low from the high doses of medication, she developed a high fever, and her contractions were now one minute apart.

"What's it from?" I asked.

"An infection," the OB answered. "Possibly from the shark attack."

There was a good chance that she was going to deliver soon,

so the doctor administered a steroid shot, an injection given to help the baby's lungs develop quickly. When a baby is born prematurely, its lungs are often not fully developed.

Dawn's condition was deteriorating rapidly, and fearing the worst, the doctor said to a nurse, "Call for a helicopter."

"Where am I going?" Dawn asked.

"I want to transport you to Good Samaritan Hospital in West Palm Beach. It's a hospital that specializes in premature and complicated births."

"Hang in there. It will be all right!" I told Dawn.

Dawn looked worried, but I knew that she wasn't about to quit. Time was of the essence, so she was quickly transferred to a stretcher and taken to the helicopter pad. When she arrived, the emergency medical flight crew was waiting. They grabbed the stretcher and began loading her onto the helicopter. I sat in my car and watched in total disbelief as she was flown away.

"Will this ever end?" I thought.

Ahead of me was a two-hour drive to Good Samaritan Hospital. I rushed to get there, hoping that I wouldn't miss the delivery. Dawn needed me and I didn't want to let her down. When I arrived at the hospital, she was already in a birthing room. Her bed was located in the center of the room. The room was enormous with all of the conveniences of home, even a bed for me. I looked and saw that she was already on a monitor with several IV lines attached. She was in labor, and her face would turn red every time she had a contraction.

"Hi, Dawn," I said.

Although I think I startled her, she was relieved to see me. I grabbed a chair and sat next to her, as we both watched the baby monitor intently, praying that her contractions would decrease. Dawn was only seven months pregnant and the doctor wanted to do everything possible to avoid a premature delivery. Her plan was to raise the amount of magnesium oxide being administered. Although the doctor hoped that the increased dosage would slow down her contractions, this was a plan not without danger. The concern was that high levels of magnesium oxide could saturate her blood and affect her ability to breathe. Because of this, Dawn's blood was drawn every four hours and checked for saturation levels, and her vital signs were monitored closely.

At first it seemed like they were experimenting-trying to find the correct dosage. Dawn's medication was raised every few hours while we waited and watched the baby monitor, hoping the medication would work. Early the next morning, her contractions finally slowed down to an acceptable amount (four to five contractions per hour) but Dawn's blood saturation level began to rise, so the doctor ordered the medication lowered. Her contractions then increased, however, so the medication was raised once again. Dawn remained on a high dosage level for several days, and that's when her health became compromised. She was lying in bed one morning in a daze, helplessly staring at the nurse making her normal rounds. Dawn wanted to say something to her, but couldn't - she felt paralyzed.

All of a sudden, she couldn't breathe. She tried to signal the nurse, but couldn't move.

"Look at me...!" she thought.

The nurse didn't notice her. Dawn was panic stricken.

"...Turn around. Look at me!" She still couldn't speak.

Then the nurse heard her sputtering to catch her breath and turned around. She quickly ran to Dawn and flushed her IV with clear fluids, restoring her ability to breathe. Dawn's blood was checked for saturation levels, and when the results came back they were extremely high - way above normal acceptance levels.

The doctor knew she had to wean Dawn off this medication, but every time her dosage was lowered, Dawn's contractions would return. I hated watching the whole process. It was so against Dawn's nature to just lie there day after day heavily medicated, not saying a word. I don't know how she survived the ordeal. It seemed so unbearable.

The doctor began to slowly wean Dawn off the magnesium oxide drip by using high levels of Brethine delivered by a pump, a device that was attached to Dawn's leg by a subcutaneous IV line that automatically pumped Brethine into her system. I remember one of the nurses commenting about the levels of medication Dawn was taking.

"If she weren't in such good physical condition, she would never be able to handle such large doses," the nurse said.

Each week that passed helped the baby's chances of survival. The doctor set short-term goals, hoping to reach a safety zone for delivery. After several more nerve racking weeks, Dawn's condition began to stabilize, and finally, the doctor gave Dawn permission to go home.

"I'll send you home on one condition," the doctor said.

"What is it?" Dawn asked.

"That you don't leave your bed. The only exceptions are to eat, shower, or go to the bathroom."

Dawn nodded her head in excitement. The next morning, a nurse showed up with a home monitoring device for contractions, and gave Dawn instructions on how to use it.

"Twice a day, we want you to place this belt around your stomach for one hour. The belt will record your uterine activity. When you're finished, place the belt on this receiver, hook it to your phone, and send the recording to our nursing station to be analyzed. They will call back telling you how many contractions you've had. You're allowed three contractions per hour."

"What if I have more?" Dawn asked.

"You'll have to give yourself a bolus (a large dosage) through your IV pump and monitor yourself for another hour."

A short time later, Dawn was transported to our home in Floridana Beach by ambulance. We now lived in a three bedroom split plan one block from the beach. When Dawn arrived home, she was surprised to see the living room set up like a birthing room, including a hospital bed as part of the decor. I can still visualize the look on Dawn's face that day. She was lying on the hospital bed smiling, even after all that she had been through.

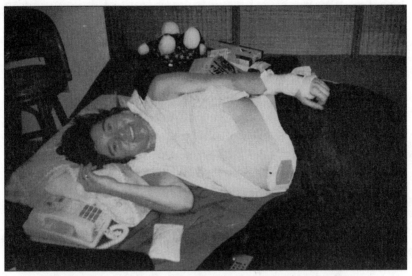

Dawn on bed rest monitoring her contractions at home

Weeks passed and our spirits were on the rise, anticipating that Dawn might be off bed rest soon but, unfortunately, on Christmas Day, Dawn's contractions broke through the medication again. Dawn administered bolus after bolus of Brethine to herself through the IV pump, but the medication didn't work. I rushed Dawn back to Good Samaritan Hospital, hoping they could stop her contractions. When we arrived she was given a shot of Brethine, but that didn't seem to work either. After spending Christmas Day lying in the hospital, Dawn began to stabilize. She was released late Christmas evening, and once again we returned home, hoping and praying this would be our last trip to West Palm Beach.

On January 11th, Dawn was finally taken off her medication and bed rest. It had been the longest thirty seven weeks of our lives, testing us both emotionally and physically. As soon as Dawn came off the Brethine pump, her uterus began to contract. At first the contractions were slow, but on January 13th they began to increase. I was surfing in front of the house with a good friend of mine, Rick, when I saw Dawn appear at the Floridana Beach pavilion . She was waving at me to come in.

"It's finally time!" I said out loud.

Dawn called the doctor, and was told not to go to the hospital until her water had broken or until her contractions were less then five minutes apart. At four o'clock in the morning on the 14th, Dawn's water broke. Unbelievably, she went back to bed without waking me. At six in the morning, she woke me up.

"It's time to go," she said in a calm voice.

"Are you sure?" I asked half asleep.

"My water broke a couple of hours ago."

I shot out of bed.

"What! Why didn't you wake me?"

"I wanted you to get a good night's sleep. Besides, we have plenty of time."

"You're crazy!" I said.

Then she insisted on eating breakfast.

After pacing back and forth for several nerve racking minutes, I said, "Let's Go!"

Dawn finally finished her cereal, and I hurried her out the door and into our pickup truck. We took off and sped down A1A toward the hospital. She looked so content sitting next to me, but her large belly was dropping with every contraction, and it made me nervous.

"I hope we make it!" I thought to myself.

When we arrived at Indian River Memorial Hospital, Dawn was taken to delivery in a wheel chair. She was assigned to the same birthing room that we had during our Thanksgiving visit.

"You're back again!" a nurse said with a familiar smile.

The baby monitor was quickly attached to Dawn's stomach, and it was confirmed that her contractions were less then three minutes apart.

The doctor came in and asked, "Do you want any pain medication?"

"No, thank you," Dawn responded.

She wanted to experience the birth naturally.

As Dawn's contractions got closer and closer together, I sat in a chair next to her thinking about all that she had been through. Dawn never screamed, but I could tell she was in excruciating pain. When she was completely dilated the doctor came in for delivery.

"Bear down with each contraction," he told her.

She pushed with all her might over and over again. I thought for sure she was going to pass out, it looked so painful and exhausting. Then at 10:30 in the morning on January 14th, 1994, Dawn delivered our son, Macintyre William Shark. He weighed 7 pounds and was 19 3/4 inches long.

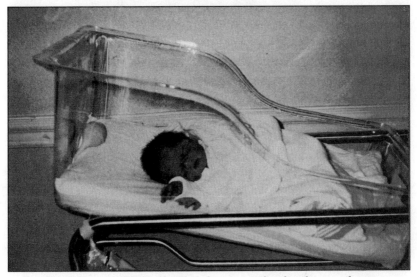

Macintyre William Shark Schauman the day he was born

Macintyre was handed to me first, while the doctor finished working on Dawn. I held him in my arms and looked into his big dark brown eyes. I wondered if he knew or felt the trauma of the shark attack. He was beautiful, and to hold him in my arms made me appreciate life and my relationship with Dawn.

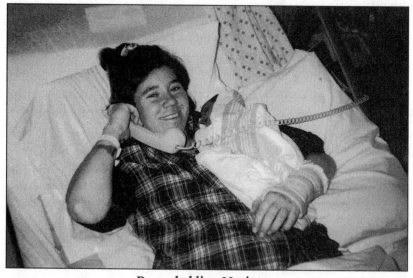

Dawn holding Macintyre

The doctor finished with the delivery of the placenta and I was finally able to hand Macintyre Shark Schauman over to Dawn. She was extremely weak from the delivery, but looked so proud with Macintyre nestled in her arms. I watched Dawn that day, her eyes filled with tears of joy, as she focused on our newborn child. I believe Dawn knew all along that Macintyre would be OK... Somebody had to be looking over her. She must have one heck of a guardian angel!

Chapter 17

After the shark attack and delivery of Macintyre, it took Dawn quite awhile to reenter the ocean. I'll never forget the first time she went back in. I had just gotten home from a quiet night at work. I parked my pickup truck in the back yard, grabbed my duffel bag, and walked through the front door.

"I'm home!" I yelled.

Dawn came rushing out of the bedroom with Macintyre in her arms, and said, "Daddy's home!"

Macintyre was now three months old. His whole face lit up with joy as I put my bag down and gave them a giant hug and kiss.

"What have you guys been doing?" I asked, lifting Macintyre playfully in the air.

While I was cuddling Macintyre in my arms, Dawn said, "We have a big surprise for Daddy today, don't we."

"What is it?" I asked.

"I've arranged for a babysitter, and you and I are going to the beach," she said. Dawn had on her red bathing suit and looked so excited.

"The babysitter won't be here until eleven, so you'll have plenty of time to play with Macintyre before she arrives."

"All right!" I said, while spinning Macintyre in the air.

The babysitter arrived promptly at eleven, and after Dawn gave her some last minute instructions, we got our bikes and left for the beach. It was a beautiful weekend day. The sun was shining brightly and the smell of blossoming trees permeated the air.

We crossed A1A, rode through the dirt parking lot and down the concrete path to the pavilion. We parked our bikes, then walked over the boardwalk to the beach.

"What a perfect beach day," I said, inhaling the fresh salt air. The water looked crystal clear and there were fishermen, sun-bathers, and people already in the water. We walked down to the water and got our feet wet. It was warm.

"Great idea!" I said looking off at the horizon.

Then, surprisingly, while she was watching several children playing in the surf, Dawn said, "Let's go swimming!"

I turned towards her and grabbed both of her hands.

"Are you sure?"

"I want to go," she said firmly.

"Ok, lets go."

She definitely wanted to face the ocean head on. I let go of her hands and waded into the water.

Dawn quickly caught up and said, "Hold my hand."

It took me back, and I wondered again if it was too soon. We continued to slowly walk out.

"Aaaahhhh!" she screamed, while leaping into my arms.

Nearly frightened to death and thinking that she had been bitten by a shark again, I yelled, "What's wrong?"

She was sobbing in my arms, and was so terrified that she couldn't answer me right away. I quickly carried her to shore - she seemed so little.

When she calmed down, I asked again, "What was it?"

"I stepped on a fish and it wiggled under my foot."

I don't think I fully understood the emotional impact of the shark attack until that moment.

About a week later she wanted to try surfing, but this time I was leery.

"Don't rush it," I told her.

"I have to," she insisted.

We jumped into the ocean together. While paddling out,

Dawn stayed so close to me that it made me nervous. I watched her catch several waves. She was jittery at first, but as the surf session went on, she seemed to regain her confidence.

"Hooo, hoo," she yelled in excitement as she rode a wave all the way to the beach.

Riding the waves seemed to take her mind off her situation. She looked so happy. You could see it in her smile. She was grinning from ear to ear.

I think the creatures of the sea will always have an unusual attraction for Dawn. One day, about a year after her shark attack, Dawn and I went fishing for Spanish Mackerel with our friend, Dave. He had a 22-foot, center-console, fishing boat. We stopped just north of the Sebastian Inlet to bait our hooks. Dave and I were going to fish off the stern, while Dawn steered the boat. We baited our hooks with live finger mullet. I threw my line overboard while Dawn stood on the seat waiting for the signal to proceed. As soon as my bait hit the water, it began swimming in circles when, suddenly, a four-foot barracuda grabbed my bait and took off. I tried to reel in the slack on my line in an effort to set the hook, but the barracuda disappeared, and then, out of nowhere, it charged. Dave and I watched in shock as the barracuda jumped completely out of the water flying across the boat. It flew right in front of Dawn's face with it's large K-9 teeth showing. She didn't have to say a word; the look on her face said it all. Dawn keeps life interesting and I never know what to expect next.

Four years after the shark attack, Dawn, who was six months pregnant with our third child, was invited to tell her story on a television program that was to be aired worldwide. It was a typical sunny day when the film crew showed up at the house. There were three of them, a director, cameraman, and sound person.

"We'd like to film at the same location as your attack," the director said.

"That's not a problem. It's only eight miles south of here," Dawn explained.

"Great," he replied.

We jumped into the pickup and drove to Treasure Shores Beach with the film crew following close behind. When we arrived, the film crew unloaded their equipment and we headed for the beach. We walked over the dune, and stopped at the end of the boardwalk.

"Where were you attacked?" the director asked.

"South of the tower," Dawn replied.

The director and crew took a moment to discuss their filming strategy.

"I'd like to interview you sitting on the beach with Macintyre," the director said. "Then take some shots with you, Bill, and Little Shark walking along the waters edge."

We made our way to the beach and sat near the lifeguard stand waiting for the crew to set up. After Dawn told her story, the crew broke down their equipment and set up again several hundred yards south of the tower. It was the same location where Dawn had crawled out of the water after her attack.

"I want you guys to walk toward the camera. Just act natural," the director said.

We walked up and down the beach five times before we were instructed to stop.

Then, when we thought we were finished, the director asked, "Dawn, would you be willing to swim in the ocean for us?"

I was dumfounded.

"He has to be kidding," I thought to myself.

"You don't have to do this," I told her.

"I know," she answered.

Although I was frightened for her and our unborn child, I knew Dawn was going to do it - she had to. She hesitated a moment.

"Yes, of course," Dawn told the director.

She walked down to the water, panned the area for any signs of sharks or bait fish.

"It's safe," she said to herself. "And the water is clear."

Dawn was still convinced she was attacked because of mistaken identity.

She put her goggles on and asked, "How far out?"

"Just beyond the breakers," the director said.

She waded out into the warm water, dove in and started swimming.

"God, please don't let anything happen to her!" I prayed.

She stopped at the location of the attack and adjusted her goggles. I wondered what she was thinking... I could feel my heart racing. I was sure it frightened her, and I hoped she would come back in, but she didn't, she continued on. After completing one full lap, she swam back to shore. When she reached the beach, I grabbed her and held her tightly. She was trembling and I could feel our unborn child kicking.

Then, unbelievably, the director asked, "Dawn, would mind doing it one more time?"

I wondered if this was some kind of test.

"You're not going out again... Are you?"

"I'll do it," she told the director firmly. "But this is the last time."

"This is insane," I thought to myself. "Enough is enough."

Dawn swam back out. It was mentally exhausting to watch, but when she returned this time, it was finally over.

On the way home we talked about the shark attack. Dawn has always been able to tell me anything.

"The ocean will always be a big part of my life," she said. "But I don't know if I'll ever feel the same about swimming in it."

To this day she jumps if anything hits her leg. Even when I go in, it doesn't feel quite the same.

Chapter 18

M y thoughts returned to the present. It was September 14th, 1998. Twenty of the longest minutes of my life had just gone by. The last time I saw Dawn, the doctor was pushing her into the operating room unconscious and pregnant with our third child. Suddenly, the hospital door to the birthing room slammed open and Dawn's doctor walked in. I studied the expression on his face, looking for an answer. His operating gown showed signs of a battle.

"You have a healthy baby boy," he said without hesitation.

"What about Dawn?" I asked.

He paused with a sigh, gaining his composure...

"She's OK!"

"Dawn had a rough time, but she'll pull through. Dawn's tough."

I looked deep into the doctor's eyes. I could see it in his face and hear it in the tone of his voice. He was as relieved as I. We both knew how close it had been, but neither one of us said a word. I shook his hand and thanked him. He never smiled. He turned without saying anything and left the room. I broke down and cried.

"Thank you, God, for the miracle that has taken place tonight!"

Dawn was safe, but she had lost a lot of blood. Our third child, Keegan John Schauman was alive and had survived a near fatal mishap. The door opened and Kelli walked in. As I hugged her with all my might, she looked at me apprehensively.

"How's Dawn?" she asked.

"The doctor just left. He said Dawn and the baby are Ok, but

I haven't seen them yet."

Kelli and I walked down the empty corridor to the waiting room. I saw Dawn's dad and brother, Wayne, sitting on the couch. I tried to explain what had been happening, but I don't think they fully understood the crucial events that had taken place. A nurse came in and escorted us to the infant intensive care unit to see Keegan for the first time. I didn't know what to expect. We were led into a small room with one mobile infant care unit sitting in the center. It was fully equipped with a bed, heating lamp, oxygen, IV pole, and numerous monitoring devices. Keegan was lying flat on his back, naked, and screaming as loud as he could. Twenty minutes ago I was ready to make a choice, and now my newborn son was lying in front of me with tubes attached to his body. I felt guilty, relieved, and concerned, all at the same time. Keegan was my fifth child and my third with Dawn. This birth had been the worst and yet, somehow, the most enlightening experience of my life.

I touched his feet. Keegan was such a big baby. He had to be at least nine pounds. He appeared to be looking toward me.

"Keegan, are you all right?"

I wondered if he recognized my voice. I'm not sure.

I turned to the nurse and said, "Dawn wants to breast feed him. It's important."

Keegan needed his mom and, most of all, I knew Dawn wanted desperately to hold her baby boy.

"Can I see Dawn?" I asked one of the nurses.

"She's in recovery, but I'll see what I can do," she replied.

Several minutes later, Dawn's dad, her brother Wayne, and I were escorted to the recovery room. It was a large room with several nurses milling around. When we walked in Dawn was lying down. I examined her face. She was not herself. Dawn always looked in control, but not this time. She was out of it and her head was swaying from side to side.

"How are you feeling?" I asked her.

Although I don't think she heard me, I know she saw me. It took her several minutes to focus.

She worriedly asked, "How's the baby?"

She wanted to hear the outcome from me, knowing that I wouldn't pull any punches.

"He's going to be all right... He's so big!"

Dawn tried to focus on me again and managed a smile, but this time her smile was different. Something had changed. I could see it and feel it. Maybe she realized for the first time how fragile life was. She actually had to rely on someone else in a life-threatening situation. It had to be the feeling of having no control over her own body. I think it frightened her, even though she would never admit it. I said a prayer that night when Dawn drifted off to sleep.

"God, I know now it was you watching over Dawn."

Chapter 19

The next morning when I arrived at the hospital, I went straight to Keegan. His condition was being monitored closely because of the emergency C- section, and he was still lying with an IV line attached to his body. Keegan was crying from hunger and desperately needed his mother's attention. It upset me knowing that he hadn't been breast fed yet. I wanted to pick him up and hold him, and tell him that everything was going to be all right.

"When can he be taken to Dawn?" I asked the nurse.

While checking Keegan's vital signs, she said, "After the pediatrician finishes her examination... He'll be OK!"

The nurse took a Polaroid picture of Keegan and said, "Give this to Dawn."

I went into Dawn's room not knowing what her condition would be. Last night she was out of it, but now she was awake, anxiously waiting to see Keegan. I walked in and gave her a kiss, then handed her the Polaroid picture of Keegan.

"He's doing good!" I assured her.

As she stared at the picture, her eyes filled with tears. I grabbed her and gave her a big hug.

After several minutes passed, I asked her if she remembered what had happened the night Keegan was delivered. Dawn told me she had temporarily regained consciousness upon entering the operating room. She could see the doctor was obviously stressed, and it frightened her.

"I'm OK!" she had told him, and attempted to assist the doctor and nurse as they lifted her onto the operating table.

Then she began fading in and out of consciousness. She

remembered lying on the operating table in a daze listening to the activity around her. There was a bright light shining in her face. The tension in the room was unbearable, and Dawn could hear nurses scurrying around cursing under their breath. Her mind drifted back to the birthing room before she passed out. She recalled the baby's monitor going off, signaling that the baby was in distress. This made her anxious, knowing that time was running out for her unborn child.

Dawn felt completely helpless and at the mercy of the doctor and nurses.

Then she heard the doctor ask, "How much longer?"

A nurse responded, "Two minutes!"

More precious time passed and still no baby!

The doctor asked again, "How much longer?" He was waiting for the anesthesiologist to arrive.

"Two minutes," the nurse said again.

Then the Doctor said, "Dawn, I'm sorry. I can't wait any longer!!"

Dawn remembered feeling intense pain and a jolt throughout her entire body. A mask was then placed over her face, and she felt as if she were about to die. She laid there helpless, wondering if she would ever see Macintyre, Casey, or me again. Dawn passed out with the thought of her precious children losing their mother.

Dawn's next conscious thought was when she woke up in recovery. Her head was swaying back and forth uncontrollably, as she tried to shake off the feeling of death. When Dawn opened her eyes and saw her father and brother standing over her, it made her think she had lost the baby. Then she focused on me. When I told her Keegan was going to be all right, she was incredibly relieved.

Just as Dawn finished telling me what had happened, the anesthesiologist walked into the room. He picked up Dawn's chart and introduced himself.

"What did you give me last night that hurt so bad?" Dawn asked.

He looked bewildered and didn't respond. The nurse who assisted with the surgery walked in, and the anesthesiologist left the room without answering Dawn's question.

The nurse overheard what Dawn had asked and said,"The pain you felt was from the doctor cutting your stomach open before you were given anesthesia...He had no choice! Time was running out and he couldn't wait any longer."

The nurse looked emotional and said, "You and the baby are very lucky to be alive!"

After the nurse left, Dawn was overwhelmed knowing what had happened. It hit her hard, as she realized for the first time how extremely close it had been. I took her in my arms as she broke down and cried.

Finally, after several hours, Keegan was brought in to breast-feed. A nurse wheeled a still very upset Keegan to Dawn's bedside, picked him up, and placed him on Dawn's chest. He instantly calmed down and began to nurse. I can still picture her lying in bed with Keegan. Although she was pale and totally exhausted, she was still able to comfort her newborn child.

Dawn had taken the brunt of the trauma and was in dire need of a blood transfusion. After discussing her options with the doctor she decided against it, learning that a transfusion might have an adverse affect on Keegan. Her decision would make the recovery process that much longer. After several days in the hospital, Dawn and Keegan were released to recover at home. The doctor instructed her to take high doses of iron and to eat blood building food such as liver. As we left the hospital, I wondered if Dawn had the physical and emotional strength to pull through.

I took the next nine days off to help. Although Dawn was extremely tired and had to literally force herself to breast-feed, she never complained.

After five days of barely being able to move, Dawn said, "Let's take a walk."

It was a gorgeous day, with a warm southeast breeze coming off the ocean. I loaded Casey and Keegan into the double stroller as Macintyre happily jumped onto his bike. We took off down Floridana Avenue as a family for the first time since Keegan's birth. Dawn struggled as she slowly hobbled beside the stroller, still in her night gown. It was hard to believe that before Keegan was born, she used to run sprints down that same road, training for triathlons.

After walking half a block, I asked, "How are you feeling?" Dawn's eyes filled with tears.

"I've never felt so weak," she said. "We'd better go back."

I felt so badly for her, but I knew she wouldn't give up.

After months of recovery, with the help of neighbors, friends, and a lot of prayers, Dawn began to show signs of improvement. Her blood count was beginning to rise and her strength was returning. She started to train on a regular basis and, before too long, could run around the block without stopping. Dawn was making a comeback, and as each day passed, her spirits began to rise.

My Dawn - my soul mate - was going to be all right!

Epilogue

D awn has since returned to a specialist to have the injuries to her hand and leg evaluated. It was determined, after two years of physical therapy and two operations to her hand, which included the removal of a bone in her left wrist, that she had sustained permanent damage. To this day, she does not have full grip strength or mobility in her

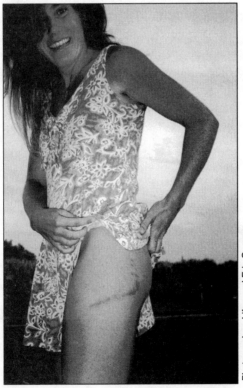

Photographer: Lifeguard Eric Carson

What Dawn's shark attack scar looks like today

left hand. Her leg also has permanent nerve damage and is numb at the site of the injury. The emotional trauma Dawn suffered cannot be measured. Every night, for a year and a half, she would wake up at three o'clock in the morning in a cold sweat. She relived the shark attack over and over again in her mind. Dawn doesn't talk about it much anymore, and I believe she is learning to cope. She is a very strong person, but now realizes that she is not invincible.

Being an active beach lifeguard was Dawn's passion, but something has changed. She has decided to give it up for a new challenge. Dawn wants to stay home and raise our children. We believe spending quality time with them is more important than anything. Dawn has become a great role model and mother to our children, and it shows.

Dawn with our children Keegan, Casey, and Macintyre

My son, from my first marriage, William Fred Schauman, is now 27 years old. He recently graduated from Whittier Law School and passed the California Bar. His ambition is to open a private law practice in Southern California. Bill and I have always been close and he is still a very important part of my life. We contact each other at least once a week by phone, and whenever the opportunity presents itself, we see each other. Bill still can't beat me at basketball, even though he has more talent. He says it's because I never let him win as a child. He also enjoys playing with his younger brothers and sister over the holidays, and considers Florida home.

Bill, Kelli, Billy, and Macintyre

Kelli, my oldest daughter, lives in Vero Beach. She is 25 years old. She and I have similar personalities, even though she hates to admit it. Her younger brothers and sister love to play with her, and are fascinated by the tattoo on her ankle. Kelli is very intuitive, always sticks up for the underdog, is artistic, loves doing her own thing, and has a heart of gold. Someday, she will be very successful at whatever she chooses to do.

Macintyre William Shark Schauman is now seven years old. He is a fun loving first grader, who loves to tell his shark story at show and tell. Mac is a very sensitive and caring child. His favorite pastimes are playing soccer, Irish step dancing, playing with his friends, and, of course, body boarding at the beach with his mom and me. Little Sharky is so coordinated he could be a great surfer someday, and recently learned how to catch sea gulls just like his mom.

Macintyre holding Keegan

Our daughter Casey

Our daughter, Casey, is now five years old and knows how to get what she wants, especially from her dad. She enjoys singing, ballet, playing dress up, baby dolls, watching television, and most of all, loves playing with her brothers and sister. At the dinner table, we all hold hands as Casey sings the family grace. She insists!

Keegan is a husky two year old who resembles a bull in a china shop. He's all boy. Keegan constantly plays with trucks and cars, loves to wrestle, and is now developing his own

Keegan

Keegan

personality. Keegan is sensitive and caring, but lets nobody push him around, not even our dog Diamond. In the evening, Dawn and I look forward to reading the kids bedtime stories, and saying our family prayers together.

Dawn wants to put her shark encounter and her lifeguard experience to good use, and hopes to become the Worldwide Lifeguard through the use of the internet. Dawn intends to send a message to beach-goers around the world that the ocean is safe, but shark attacks can happen. To help accomplish her mission, she has developed a web site called SharkSurvivor.com. Dawn and other shark attack victims, along with shark experts, will be interviewed to provide an insight into why shark attacks occur, and how they can possibly be prevented. The sharks that coincide with the interviews will be illustrated and described to provide a better understanding of their behavior. Dawn believes that certain sharks are aggressive by nature, but that most attacks occur due to mistaken identity. The site will also supply tips on possible ways to avoid a shark attack, and how Dawn personally survived.

Dawn's most innovative creation on the site is her Lifeguard Safety Board. Lifeguard agencies and dedicated volunteers worldwide will be able to post daily ocean safety conditions and special hazards for beach-goers on hometown Lifeguard Safety Boards. Finally, she plans to set up a Memorial Board for deceased shark attack victims. The Memorial Board will reveal the magnitude of what can happen and how important it is to understand ocean conditions and possible hazards. Dawn hopes that by creating a coalition of environmental stewardship and an increased knowledge about ocean safety conditions and shark behavior, people and sharks will be able to coexist.

Today, Dawn is happy with her life. She is still able to raise our children at home and, despite her busy schedule, always puts them first. Dawn loves teaching Irish Step Dancing to our children and the neighborhood kids, swimming, surfing, working out at the gym, running, basketball, volleyball, and, most of all, spending time alone with the family in the Tennessee mountains.

When Dawn's happy, everything seems right. I can't wait to come home from work, just to see her and our children playing in the driveway. I don't think Dawn will ever grow up. At least I hope not. She is content just doing her own thing and doesn't care what anyone thinks. Dawn fascinates me. She always will. We're lovers and best friends.

Forever!!